Psalms in Poetry

The Rhythm and Rhyme
of HOPE

Psalms in Poetry

The Rhythm and Rhyme
of HOPE

by Keith W. Currie

W H P
Wyatt House Publishing
www.wyattpublishing.com
Mobile, Alabama

Wyatt House books may be ordered through booksellers or by contacting:

WYATT HOUSE PUBLISHING
399 Lakeview Dr. W.
Mobile, Alabama 36695
www.wyattpublishing.com

Because of the dynamic nature of the Internet, any web address or links contained in this book may have changed since publication and may no longer be valid. The views expressed in this book are solely those of the author and do not necessarily reflect those of the publisher, and the publisher hereby disclaims any responsibility for them.

Cover design by: Mark Wyatt and Mary Ann Wyatt

ISBN 13 TP: 978-0-9882209-6-6
Library of Congress Control Number: 2013932740

Printed in the United States of America

Acknowledgments

A very special thanks to John Stanko, whose timely visit with our family several years ago, was a tremendous encouragement to write a book.

Of course, my wife Patricia has been a constant encouragement as she patiently listened to me excitedly read a certain Psalm or poem or expression along the way. My mom has always been my best fan, believing the best of me even when I deserved it least. Along with these two great women, my six kids (Anna, Patrick, Will, Judith, Jean-Luc, and Daniel) also threw in their occasional "That's good, Dad." Judith and Dan, in particular, often had a poem or a part of a poem for breakfast: eggs, toast, and poetry.

Also, during the time of writing, we were fortunate to share our home with Travis and later Alicia. They too had occasional poetry for breakfast.

Oliver Heath has been a longtime friend as well as a key backer for this project. Mary Kay Butler for friendship and for being willing, like the Psalmist David, to ask hard questions through the years.

Thank you to all the backers who got involved through KickStarter and propelled this project to fulfillment: Mike Reed, Ellen Giattina, Clara Courson, Edna Schuligoj, Susan Rouse, Jason Whatley, Muhammad AL-Kahlout, Leah Guillory, Cheryl Etheredge, Cheslea Popiel, Ray Notgrass, Deborah Fulgham, Leigh Ann Dismukes, Sonya Simmons Stearns, Margaret Pass, Ashlie Charest, Van Sebastian Moran, Keith Dugger, Melanie Nelson, John B. Nowell, Lisa Blackman, Mark Powell, Lisa McCollum, Ken McAuliffe, Lydia Heath, Tommy Fulton, Pam Bataller, Kim Martinez, Carol, Justin, Gloworm, Brent Cumbest, Jeff Roberts, Micah Heath, Jason Jones, Beth Moore Mullett, David Brumbaugh, Matt Etheredge, Ruth Grant, Richard Spitzkopf, Carolyn Tormala, Stephen Roberts, Christ Olson, Danica, Kay Rindahl, Maggie Thomas, Rev. Lois M. Baker, Miranda Patrick, Ronald Gray, Linda Harris, Theda Hii, Thomas Hernandez, Alicia Palmer, Jay Morgan, Lorraine Pearce, Chris Leininger, Jeremy Patrick, Tom Bagwell, Lisa Denham, Grant and Stacy Simpson.

Thanks also to Mark Wyatt, publisher and backer.

And above all, my greatest gratitude to God the Father, Son, and Holy Spirit who is Hope, and Life, and Music, and Poetry, and Love, and Power, and Justice and . . . "over all and in all and through all."

Keith W. Currie
February 2013

Psalm	Title
1	Believe It or Not
2	World Perspective
3	Saving Father
4	I Call to You
5	Morning Prayer for Favor
6	Tearful Prayer
7	Running Scared
8	Leadership Delegated
9	Because of You
10	Righteous Vengeance
11	Lovers of Right
12	Hope that Endures
13	A Dark Day
14	Foolish Choice
15	True Man
16	Treasured Life
17	A Just Hope
18	My Rock
	Holy Grit
	You Alone
	You Make Me the Head
	Enduring Rock
19	Look Up
	He Points the Way
20	Answer in Person
21	I Asked for Life

Introduction

Shorty, Billy, and Oswald combined to influence me to write this book.

Shorty was my dad, lover of songs and poems. His own spontaneity in making up little songs or poems in the moment, in teaching his three children the phrases and fun little tunes that he remembered from his own childhood: these things are with me to this day. I am not a serious student of poetry, analyzing and critiquing; but I enjoy poetry or a well-written song because of Shorty. He lived with a lilt and a laugh. He relished the experience of rhyme and rhythm. The elements of poetry I learned in school would have had little effect had it not been for Dad's way of just enjoying. The enjoyment I received in the writing of these poems were God's gift to me through Shorty.

Billy Duke is my pastor and has been a part of my life for over thirty years. How often, as he has prayed for me and encouraged me, I have recognized that his counsel and his prayer came from the Psalms. He has reminded me from Psalms 31 that "my times are in His hands." He has encouraged thanksgiving with the phrase from Psalm 16: "the lines have fallen for me in pleasant places." These prayers and heart-felt expressions of hope in God that occupy the middle of the Bible were lived out before me in Billy's life. I am grateful for his prayers and his influence. Over time, his example caused my own hope to gain more depth through the Psalms.

Oswald Chambers, best known for his book *My Utmost for His Highest*, also wrote this: "The real reason for prayer is intimacy with our Father. There are many ways that help . . . To rewrite the Psalms into a free language of expression of one's own has proved to me a valuable treasure-house of self-expression to God."

One morning as I read these words, I was challenged to do this for myself, to rewrite the Psalms in my own expression as an enhancement of my own intimacy with our Father. I was reading through the Psalms at the time; so I began where I was in my reading—with

Psalm 112. The thought to write it as poetry was my own idea. Over the next two-and-a-half years, somewhere along the way, I realized that it might become a book.

So here it is. It is my hope that you enjoy, that you are encouraged and filled with hope, and that your own intimacy with our Father is deepened and enlarged.

Psalm 1

BELIEVE IT OR NOT

How well off the one who will not walk
In the wiles of the wicked.
So safe the soul that stands aloof
From sin's Deception Street.
The soul that seeks the truth that's sound
Won't sit in a scoffing seat.
How well off the one who will not walk
In the wiles of the wicked.

Instead, he delights in the law of the Lord
And makes it his meditation.
So like a tree whose roots run deep
Nearby the river's banks,
With timely fruit and leaf that's green,
He prospers and gives thanks.
Yes, he delights in the law of the Lord
And makes it his meditation.

The wicked are like the dust in the wind;
God's breath blows them away.

They'll fade from sight on Judgment Morn
When truth shines strong and bright,
For sinners cringe in righteous crowds
And hide from holy light.
The wicked are like the dust in the wind;
God's breath blows them away.

Psalm 2

WORLD PERSPECTIVE

Why have the nations gone so insane
And made their policies force?
And the people's plans are plainly vain;
They've chosen Failure's Course.

A summit's called for heads of state
To sit around the table.
Deceived by sudden rise to power,
They feel that they are able
To solve the problems without God
With treaties, pacts, and such;
But when the meeting's said and done,
It really wasn't much.

God sits in heaven and He laughs,
Amused at all their bluster.
From there He speaks His living-word
That leaves their plans afluster.

In purposed anger, He'll declare
That Jesus is the King,
The Son begotten before time
And from whom all things spring.

He'll place the nations in His hands--
Every single one.
His iron decrees will rule them all;
Their own laws come undone.

So kings, show wisdom; judges, learn
And tremble at His throne.
Show highest honor to the Son,
To Him and Him alone.

For wrath awaits those who refuse
To see Him as He is;
But blessing waits for those who yield
And gladly become His.

Psalm 3

SAVING FATHER

Father God,
I am surrounded;
All around my enemies rise!
The word on the street
Is that I'm done for;
Everyone waits for my demise.

But Father God,
You are my shield.
You swing Your weight, exalt my head.
When I cried out from Anguish Alley,
You gave not death,
But life instead!

I lay and slept.
When I awoke,
I knew that you had saved my life.
I will not fear
when you are near,
Though thousands seek to cause me strife.

O Father, rise,
O saving God,
Who smote my foes with crushing blows,

Salvation all
Belongs to You!
O make our blessings overflow.

Psalm 4

I CALL TO YOU

O God, my Goal, my Good, my Guide,
I call to You; come take my side.
In past distress You brought relief;
Bend down to hear this prayer of grief.

It seems that men have gone insane,
Exalting evil, good profaned.
They seek the lowest, live the lie,
Keep up an image 'til they die.

The Lord has set his watchful gaze
Upon the man whose Godlike ways
Call God's attention to his prayer.
I call to Him and He is there.

Trembling awe keeps us from sin,
Stills our souls and speaks within,
"Choose Wisdom's Year, not Pleasure's Day;
Know God rewards the Waiting Way."

Many expect care only from men;

Lord, show Your favor once again.
You satisfy; my heart takes wings.
But not for temporary things.

You are my Home, the place I dwell;
My place of rest, where I sleep well.
O God, my Goal, my Good, my Guide,
I call to You; come take my side.

Psalm 5

MORNING PRAYER FOR FAVOR

I speak, I groan, I cry for help;
In the morn, I pray, I lift my voice.
I order my prayer to You and watch
To trust You is my only choice.

What kinds of things do You despise?
The boastful will not catch Your eyes;
The evil plot, the wicked plan,
The violent and deceitful man
Who speaks with false and flattering tongue,
Much like a ladder's broken rung.
Rebellious, he ignores your call;
By his own devices let him fall.

But as for me, I'm bowing down
And mercy meets me at your gate.
I join in joyful song with those

Who've refuged in Your love so great.

Spread Your protection over us.
Your name we love, Your Presence savor.
O bless this righteous man, O Lord,
Surround him with your shield of favor.

Psalm 6

TEARFUL PRAYER

O Lord,
> Your nostrils are flared
> In anger towards me!
> It poisons my body,
> Sickens my soul.

O Lord,
> Stoop down and see
> I'm wasting away;
> Withdraw your wrath
> And make me whole.

O Lord,
> What good am I dead?
> No thanks on my lips,
> Your name never praised. . .
> Grant me relief.

O Lord,
    I've cried so much
    My bed should float;
    My chair is soaked
    Because of grief.

O Lord,
    Set me apart
    From iniquitous men.
    Turn enemies back;
    Turn them to shame.

O Lord,
    You've heard me weep.
    You've heard me ask.
    You've heard me pray.
    I praise Your name.

Psalm 7

RUNNING SCARED

Like a deer, I'm running;
For dear life, I'm running;
From evil, I'm running;
Running to You.

If I have done evil,
Or my hands done evil,

If I've done my friend evil,
If I've been unjust,

Let me be chased by evil,
And be caught by evil,
And flattened by evil,
And trampled to dust.

O Lord, with Your anger,
Your tsunami of anger,
Wash enemy anger
Far out to sea.

When the peoples are judged,
And my enemies judged,
And when I am judged,
Lord, vindicate me.

Now evil brings death,
No repentance brings death,
And violence brings death,
The weapon of God.

A pit is a trap,
A hole is a trap,
When a man sets a trap,
He's the one who gets caught.

My shield is the Lord,
I give thanks to the Lord,
I sing praise to the Lord,
To Jesus, Most High!

Psalm 8

RULERSHIP DELEGATED

Your incredible majesty can be seen
From anywhere on earth!
The splendor of the skies display
Your great creative mirth.

In every country, every land,
Your testimonies rise,
And babbling infants in their joy
Refute the atheist's lies.

I view the heavens, moon and stars
In vast ordained design,
And wonder fills my heart to think
You care for humankind.

You've shared with us Your spirit life
And crowned us as your kin
To rule the earth, the skies, the seas,
And all the beasts therein.

Your incredible majesty can be seen
Everywhere on earth.

Psalm 9

BECAUSE OF YOU

Heartfelt thanksgiving!
    Wonder-filled witness!
        Gladness, rejoicing!
            Praise to You!

Enemies stumble,
    Enemies back up,
        Enemies perish
            Because of You.

Righteous judgment,
    Widespread justice,
        Great jubilation,
            Come from You.

The wicked destroyed,
    The wicked ruined,
        Gone forever
            Because of You.

Abiding always,
    Unassailable,
        Unconquerable refuge,
            We seek You.

Never forsaking,
      Never forgetting,
            Ever forgiving,
                  Gracious are You!

Nations? Mere men.
      Self-seeking men,
            God-shunning men.
                  Our judge is You.

Sing to the Lord,
      Declare to the earth
            The flourishing goodness
                Given by You.

Psalm 10

RIGHTEOUS VENGEANCE

JE-SU-U-U-US! WHERE ARE YOU?

The wicked pursue me with trouble in hand.
Let them trip in their traps, in the plots they have planned.

JE-SU-U-U-US! WHERE ARE YOU?

The wicked men boast; the greedy men curse,
Treat God like a myth, grow increasingly worse.
Yet he prospers so much, seems strong in his health.

He fears not his foes; he's secure in his wealth.
He will curse and deceive, plan mischief and guile;
And lurking, he waits for the innocent child.
Like a cat waits for prey, he is crouched for the pounce,
And the unwary soul gets unmercifully trounced.
He has no thought of God, no fear and no guilt;
For he thinks God can't see through the walls he has built.

Jesus is King; and the tyrants that rise
Have illusions of power, then meet their demise.
To the humble, give ear. To the orphan, give rest.
And deal with the tyrant who cruelly oppressed.

God certainly sees, and surely He works
To avenge every babe that the wicked have hurt.

Psalm 11

LOVERS OF RIGHT

The Lord is my Protector;
I will not run and hide.
For the wicked is about
With a weapon by his side
To spread his darkness over men
And rule them in his pride.
So I must stand for right and truth;
The wrong must be defied.

From where God dwells, He sees it all
And views the deeds of men.
He grants them what they love the most
Again and yet again:

Lovers of war will get their fill
Of violence, death, and pain.
Lovers of right will get the thrill
Of God's good, righteous reign.

Psalm 12

HOPE THAT ENDURES

O Lord, our Hope:
    Godly men have gone away
    And faithful men have failed to stay
    To fight the evil of this day.

How lies abound!
    The language of the day is lies;
    And double-meanings just disguise
    The plans of those who tyrannize.

The devil's plot:
    Chameleon-like through crowds, he slips
    To keep them in his devious grips
    By vacuous vows and flattering lips.

The wicked's lust:

When men desire the lowest smut,
The wicked walks with arrogant strut
And gleefully gluts his lustful gut.

Our only Hope:
>The needy groans, the poor man sighs,
>Each innocent weeps, for safety cries,
>"Til God says, "Now I will arise!"

Our only Strength:
>The words of the Lord are tried and pure;
>His Presence near, His promise sure,
>To grace His people to endure.

Psalm 13

A DARK DAY

Am I out of the loop? Am I being ignored?
Have you hidden your face from your servant, O Lord?
I counsel myself; but my reasoning's skewed;
My heart is in pain; and my hope is subdued.

I despair because of my enemy's laugh,
For he's putting to paper my epitaph.
But it's not yet in stone; not if You look my way:
Give life to my soul for yet one more day.

I have placed myself in Your steadfast love,
And my heart awaits joy in Your help from above.
I will sing, I will shout, I will dance when I'm free
Because You, O my Lord, have been gracious to me.

Psalm 14

FOOLISH CHOICE

"There is no God!" "There is no God!"
The fool repeats as if to say,
"Repeat it enough; he'll go away!"
"There is no God!" "There is no God!"

Their appetites become their gods.
They soon corrupt for selfish needs;
Commit the vilest, foulest deeds.
Their appetites become their gods.

Do any do good? Do any seek God?
The Lord looks on the sons of man
To find just one who understands.
Do any do good? Do any seek God?

They're all astray; they're all corrupt.
Not one does good, not even one!
NOT ONE DOES GOOD, NOT EVEN ONE!
They're all astray; they're all corrupt.

They never call upon the Lord;

Avoiding mention of His name,
Headlong they rush to dust and shame.
They never call upon the Lord.

A refuge for the righteous man:
Salvation's only source is Christ.
And restoration's force is Christ:
A refuge for the righteous man.

Psalm 15

TRUE MAN

Who lives with you, O Lord the Just?
What kind of person earns your trust?

The one whose deed and word concur,
Who values others and defers.

Who speaks no slander, won't encroach,
Protects his friend from false reproach.

The reprobate, his eyes deplore;
He honors those who fear the Lord.

He walks with friends through sacrifice.
He keeps his word and pays a price.

He gladly lends, no hope of gain;
He can't be bribed: lets justice reign.

His heart of truth cannot be taken.
This kind of man cannot be shaken!

Psalm 16

TREASURED LIFE

Hold me in Your hands, O God,
My refuge, strong, secure.
O Lord, You are my only good
Alone--I can't endure.

The saints who spread throughout the earth,
Majestic in their lives,
Delight my soul, rejoice my heart;
May all their families thrive.

Multiplying sorrows follow
Those who buy their gods:
Their names abominations,
Their offerings, just facades.

My endowment is the Lord
In place of heirlooms, rich and grand.
His vastness is my boundary,
My beloved fatherland.

My present state suits me quite well;
My heritage has no end.

His counsel in my darkest hour
Grants grace to comprehend.

My eyes are fixed; I look to Him.
He's near, my soul secure.
My heart is glad, my spirit laughs.
My flesh is strong and sure.

The grave will not have final say;
This soul of mine will not decay.

You show me life; You make me live!
Eternal joy You gladly give.

Your presence is my greatest treasure;
To be with You, my greatest pleasure.

Psalm 17

A JUST HOPE

I ask for justice; hear my prayer.
My lips do not deceive.
Lord, view my case and weigh the facts;
Your judgment, I'll receive.

You've tried my heart and watched my soul
As darkness I have fought.
You've tested me; but I've not voiced
A single sinful thought.

Avoiding paths of violent rogues,
I've made Your word my script.
I've kept my feet upon Your path;
And there, they have not slipped.

I've called--You've heard! O, once again
Protect Your faithful few.
In steadfast love deliver us;
Our enemies pursue!

Guard me as You would an eye;
Wrap Your wings around
From wicked ones who seek to ruin,
From enemies who surround.

Their hearts are hard; their words are proud.
They lurk, they stalk, they hide;
And then like lions who seize their prey,
They pounce from every side.

Arise, and bring him low, O Lord,
This man who brings me strife;
Confront him with Your unsheathed sword
Who lives but for this life.

His belly full, he leaves his wealth
To children when he dies.
My wealth is but to see Your face:
Your likeness as my prize.

Psalm 18

MY ROCK

I love You, Lord,
My Strength, my Rock,
My Fort, Rescuer,
God, my Rock.

My Place of Safety,
Place of Strength,
My Shield, Salvation,
God, my Rock.

I call on You;
My enemies flee!
O Worthy One,
God, my Rock.

I call on You,
O Worthy One,
My shield, salvation,
God, my Rock!

HOLY GRIT

When floods o'erwhelm, and death draws near,
My cry for help comes to Your ear.

Though earth may shake, foundations tremble,
My help comes from Your holy temple.

You come in thunder and lightning's flash;
You ride dark clouds; Your hailstones crash.

The rivers rise; the earth is split;
And evil flees from Holy Grit.

YOU ALONE

From high above He lifts me up;
I'm borne beyond the fray.
He sets me in a broader place
Where safety rules the day.

He visits me with His reward,
Commends me for my stand:
That I have kept myself from sin
And clung to His command.

Toward the kind, You are so kind;
Toward the pure, You're pure;
When one is blameless, You don't blame;
For the sick, You are the cure.

You out-think the clever,
You humble the proud;
You illumine our darkness,
Dispelling our clouds.

Your way ever blameless,
Your word strong and sure;
You're the shield on our journey;
You help us endure.

You are God, You alone!
By Your strength, You empower
And train us for battle
When foes would devour.

YOU MAKE ME THE HEAD

My feet do not slip,
For I'm in Your grip.

In meek-robe I stride,
While enemies hide.

My arm becomes strong;
I pursue all day long.

I will finish the chore
You've created me for.

I can persevere
And face every fear.

In spite of the past,
I rise to the task.

The enemy's hoax

Becomes just a joke.

The tail? No, instead,
You make me the head!

ENDURING ROCK

The Lord is alive!
Enduring Rock.

Exalted God,
Enduring Rock.

Victory Giver,
Enduring Rock.

Strong Deliverer,
Enduring Rock.

Posterity's hope,
Enduring Rock.

I'll sing Your praise,
Enduring Rock.

Psalm 19

LOOK UP

Look up!
    The sky has a secret!
        A message!
        A declaration!
        A proclamation!
            The glory of God!

Look up!
    His work is seen!
        It is heard!
        It's unveiled!
        It's revealed!
            The knowledge of God!

Look up!
    His touch is there!
        To enjoy!
        To enlighten!
        To enrich!
            The blessing of God!

No speech,
    No words,
        No sounds,
Yet His mighty message still abounds
            Throughout the earth.

HE POINTS THE WAY

He points the way to being whole:
A soul refreshed is a refreshing soul.

Recounting God's help makes our spirits rise;
And the most naive become truly wise.

Accounting to God will set us right,
Will set us free, will make hearts light.

The call of God so clarifies:
Puts truth in our souls and fire in our eyes.

Respect for God brings purity
And makes us stand in security.

God's judgments are solid, ever in tandem,
Just and right and never random;
More valued than gold in purest form
And sweeter than honey from the beehive's swarm.

There are truths that warn and sound an alarm;
There are truths that reward and bring life charm.

We all have faults that we can't see;
And we all presume to a certain degree.

Though I'm biased for self, let me learn Your ways;
Make me blameless in deeds; do not let me stray.

O be pleased with me, Father, from whom I have sprung,
With the thoughts of my heart, and the words from my
tongue.

Psalm 20

ANSWER IN PERSON

When trouble comes, so does God
With His name, His nature, His mighty arm.
Need help from heaven? A warning alarm?
Proof of approval? Protection from harm?

May He grant your desire, the cry of your heart,
Your counsel be sure, your plans fulfilled.
Sing joyful songs with victorious thrill.
Proclaiming His name with jubilant trill.

I know that the Lord will save His child;
He answers from heaven, goes any length.
Some boast weapons, some boast strength,
But man grows weary and falls full-length.

We boast in Jesus, the expression of God;
We rise from the dust, avoid death's curtain.
Save from strife; don't let things worsen.
We call on You; You answer in person.

Psalm 21

I ASKED FOR LIFE

Jesus,
When you give strength, I'm glad, I'm glad!
When you deliver, how I rejoice!

You've given me my heart's desire;
You've granted me my soul's request.
You come with blessings right and good;
You crown me with the very best.

I asked for life; You freely gave
Eternal life, everlasting days.
Because of You, I have achieved;
Respect and honor, I've received.

Your humble guest, I'm ever blest;
Your presence fills, and calms, and thrills.
O Lord Most High, I trust in You;
Your faithful love will hold me true.

Your enemies plot with ill intent;
You let them rant and rave and vent.
Emboldened by Your quiet ways,
They run the course of evil days
And brag and boast and plot and scheme
'Til all that's good is lost, it seems.

But then You rise in glorious might,
With Beauty and Truth dispel the night.
Your enemies have nowhere to hide;
The end has come to evil's tide.

When godly strength is on display,
We sing in Your eternal day.

Psalm 22

DEATH THREAT

My God! My God!
      Why leave me all alone?
I groan, I groan,
      But hope of help is gone.

I cry by day;
      You don't grant my request.
I cry by night;
      I can't get any rest.

O Holy One,
      Your people all agree:
Our fathers leaned
      On You--You set them free!

I am a worm
      Reproached, despised by men.
They shake their heads,

And mock me yet again.
"Trust God," they say,
    "Let's see Him do His stuff."
"Stand back," they say,
    "Let's see if God's enough."

You gave me life
    You drew me from the womb.
You are my God,
    My Trust from birth to tomb.

Be close at hand,
    I'm stuck in trouble's hour.
Bulls trample me,
    And roaring lions devour.
I melt like wax
    My bones like liquid pour.
My strength is gone
    And death is at the door.

I'm caught; I'm seized;
    They pierce my feet and hands
And take my clothes
    The spoils from dying man.
Be close at hand;
    Between my life and woe.
Disperse each foe,
    And death itself must go.

I'll shout Your name;
    I'll make Your praises loud!
O fear the Lord,

And join the praising crowd.
O stand in awe;
    He cares for sick and weak:
They cry for help--
    He is the Help they seek.

Praise starts in You,
    Goes out through me to men.
I keep my word,
    And walk with godly friends.

When suffering ends,
    Your seekers give You praise.
"Live on and on!"
    We shout with voices raised.

The ends of earth
    Will wake to what is true;
And hearts in homes
    Will bow and worship You.

You are the King
    Who rules the nations' towers;
Successful ones
    Acknowledge all Your powers.

In dust of death
    All men will bow the knee,
And unbelievers, too,
    Will finally see
The future's Yours.
    Those yet to come will hear;

And they'll pass on
　　　Your deeds from year to year.

Psalm 23

SHEPHERD

The Lord's my loving Shepherd;
He always will provide
Rest from striving,
Quiet release,
Strength in spirit,
Guiding peace.

In days of deathly darkness,
No evil will I fear:
You're with me
In the journey,
Nudging, leading,
Always near.

Enemies rise but You're undaunted,
Blessing me
Before their eyes,
Choosing me
To do Your bidding,
Handing me
The victor's prize.

Every day from here to always,
Goodness, mercy leave me never.
I will dwell
Within Your house.
I will live
With You forever.

Psalm 24

KING OF INFINITE GOOD

The earth is the Lord's and everything in it:
The world and its people and each passing minute.
Unique among worlds, it has oceans and seas
And rivers to water its grasses and trees.

It's an uphill climb, God's will to find;
You have to go against the flow.
Clean hands, pure heart, a soul that's true:
God's grace and presence come to you.

His blessing comes and you're made right;
His presence comes, salvation's light.
This generation longs to see
The face of God--His majesty!

Now think these thoughts
And open your hearts.
The King of Good is coming in.

Who is this King of Infinite Good?
He is also Lord of infinite power
Who never fails in the critical hour.

Now think these thoughts
And open your hearts.
The King of Infinite Good is come.

Who is this King of Infinite Good?
He is the King of Constant Help.
He is the King of Infinite Good!

Psalm 25

I AIM MY LIFE TOWARD YOU

I aim my life toward You, O Lord;
Don't let my enemies gain.
I know that I can trust in You.
Don't leave me in my pain.

Not one who waits for You, O Lord,
Will hang his head in shame.
But a treacherous one who lives for self
Will end with sullied name.

Make me know Your paths, O Lord;
Each day Your ways anew.
For You are God of life and strength;
I aim my life toward You.

Remember compassion and faithful love--
The way You've always been--
But not my iniquities, not my wrongs;
Do not recall my sin.

You are ever good and always right,
So train me not to stray.
In justice I will follow You
As children learn Your way.

The paths are truth and steadfast love,
When to You I am bound.
Your name is grace and mercy, Lord,
When wrongs in me abound.

Who is the man who fears the Lord?
Instruct him in the Way.
His soul will live and grow in grace;
His children thrive each day.

God shares His thoughts with reverent men;
He binds Himself to them.
I aim my life toward You, O Lord;
So keep my steps from sin.

Lord, look my way; be kind to me;
I'm troubled and alone.
The struggles in my heart are huge;
My words just one big groan.

Lord, look my way, and see my plight;
And pardon all my sins.

Lord, all my foes surround me now;
Their hatred does me in.

In You I'm not ashamed, O Lord.
So make my soul be true.
My heart, my deeds are in Your hands;
I aim my life towards You.

Psalm 26

NO FOG BETWEEN US

Judge me, Lord; I've walked with You.
I've trusted You, I've followed through.
Look at me, inside and out;
In mind and heart, I've been devout.
Your faithful love I've kept in sight;
I've walked with You; You've been my light.

With proud pretenders, I won't sit;
I stay far from the hypocrite.
I hate the mob of evildoers,
The crowd whose minds are reeking sewers.
I cleanse my hands to oft pursue
The kind of life that pleases You.

I love the sense that You are near;
No fog between us: all is clear.
Don't exile me with sinful throng;
Don't let me choose the crowd of wrong

Whose hands are full of wicked schemes,
Who bribe their way to futile dreams.

I offer thanks and praise as one;
I'm filled with awe at all You've done.
I'll walk in Your integrity,
And You in grace will walk with me.
I'll take my stand on solid ground
And join the crowd where praise abounds.

Psalm 27

TRUST

The Lord's my Light;
Whom shall I fear?
He's on my side;
What shall I dread?
When evil comes
To steal and kill,
I will not fear
But trust instead.

One thing I ask
And this pursue:
To know Your thoughts,
To see Your face,
For all my days
To live with You,

Kept in Your hand,
Your secret place.

You lift my head
I shout with joy.
I sing and play
My loudest chord.
My voice cries out,
"Grant grace to me!"
You say, "Draw near."
I draw near, Lord.

Don't hide Your face
Nor angry be.
You are my help;
Don't banish me.
O, Savior God,
When parents leave,
Forsake me not;
Take care of me.

Teach me Your way
And lead me true.
Don't give me up
To fiendish foes.
False witnesses
With violent breath
Rise up to harm
And breathe out woes.

I would despair
But I believe

I'll see the good
Of God the Great!
You'll give me strength
And courage too;
I'll live with trust
In You . . . and wait.

Psalm 28

I ASK, I YIELD

O Lord, my Strength, I call to You.
Lord, don't be deaf, don't pass me by.
For if You do, I'll die . . . I'll die.

I cry to You with pleading voice;
I lift my hands to heaven's throne:
"Don't leave me here alone . . . alone."

Don't cart me off with wicked men
Who snare the mob with soothing song
'Til good and right are gone . . . far gone.

Repay the work of evil men;
Repay with fires that burn and singe.
For what they've done, avenge . . . avenge.

They hate the works that You have done.
They fail to hail Your sovereign crown.
Don't build them up; tear down . . . tear down.

You've heard the pleading of my voice.
You've heard the cry of my request,
"O Lord, my God, be blessed . . . be blessed!"

O Shepherd God, our strong defense,
Do care for us; keep us from harm.
Protect us with Your arm . . . Your arm.

You are my trust; You are my song.
You are my strength; You are my shield.
My heart adores: I yield . . . I yield.

Psalm 29

KING OF ALL

If you have power and you have might,
If you have wisdom and great insight,
If you have wealth or place or fame,
Each one of these will bear His name.

You can hear His voice in the ocean's roar,
In the sound of the surf as it breaks to shore,
In the peal of thunder that rumbles and rolls,
In its sudden surprise when it shakes to the soles.
Majestic and strong, it splits the trees,
The cedars and oaks bend at their knees.
The world even wobbles like a new-born calf,
And the earth starts to split as if breaking in half.
Volcanoes erupt with ashes and flame

And the wilderness shakes as it whispers His name.
His voice evokes violence and His voice brings birth,
And His glory is shouted in this temple called earth.

In the time of the flood, the Lord was the King;
He is King evermore and He rules everything.

His strength He bestows on the people He knows;
And His peace He imparts to the people whose hearts
. . . are His.

Psalm 30

HIS FAVOR

I will lift You up, O Lord,
For You have lifted me.
You've disappointed those who wished
To see me fail and flee.

I cried to You for help, O God;
You came and gave me breath.
You saved me from the darkest pit;
You kept my soul from death.

O godly ones, give thanks, sing praise
And shout His holy name!

His favor flows for all our lives;
His anger's in and out.

Though tears may flow throughout the night,
The morning brings a shout!

When things went well, I felt so safe;
Your favor made me strong.
When pride increased, You hid Your face,
And life was veering wrong.

I called to You from on my knees;
I begged for You to save.
What profit is there in my death?
No praises from the grave.

      O godly ones, give thanks, sing praise
      And shout His holy name!

O Lord, please hear; show grace to me.
You've helped my circumstance.
You've caused my mournful, plodding feet
To prance a dapper dance.

You've taken clouds and shrouds from me
And set my heart aflame.
My soul, now free, sings endless praise,
And thanks Your holy name.

      O godly ones, give thanks, sing praise
      And shout His holy name!

Psalm 31

SOURCE OF HOPE

O eternal, faithful Refuge,
You're my castle on the crag,
High above the devil's bluster,
Over Satan's boastful brag.

From this vantage on the mountain
Vision's clear and fresh the air;
You look down upon the lowlands
Showing me each shameful snare.

Faithful Guide, my path is certain;
I'm rejoicing in Your care.
You've foreseen my fights, my struggles;
You'll be with me when I'm there.

When my stresses make me struggle,
When I waste away with woes,
When my strength has dissipated,
When I'm scorned by all my foes,
When my friends are loathe to greet me,
When they shun me lest we meet,
When I'm pushed aside, forgotten,
Terrors grasping at my feet,
Spirits whisper from the shadows
Planting death-thoughts in my head.
Strike them dumb, Eternal Guardian;
Strengthen me, but strike them dead.

A wealth of kindness You are keeping
For the ones who side with You;
In Your company they're in safety
When the slanderous stories spew.

In the midst of desperation,
I just didn't think You'd hear;
You surprised me with Your favor;
In Your faithful love appeared.

Love the Master, faithful followers,
When the proud run out of rope.
Strengthen hearts, hold on to courage;
God is still our source of hope.

Psalm 32

DON'T BE A MULE

When you own your sin,
    express your fault,
    admit your guilt,
    dismiss deceit,
    confess to God,
A spirit filled with freedom comes;
Your heart then sings, your spirit hums.

When you hide your sin,
    express no fault,
    admit no guilt,

adopt deceit,
avoid the light,
excuse yourself,
Vitality, vim, and vigor leave,
Your body fails, your conscience grieves.

When troubles come,
The rising floods,
Can reach me not.
I pray to You,
You guard my life,
Surround with aid.
You will instruct me how to choose,
My wisdom I will gain from You.

Don't be a mule
That needs a bit,
A bridled colt
That needs a jerk,
That follows not
Without a rope.
God's favor falls if you will trust;
You'll shout for joy--strong and robust!

Psalm 33

IN HIM WE BOAST

Rejoice! Rejoice! Sing songs of praise;
That fits the souls that God has raised.
Guitars, zitars, play from the heart,
Or chord the keyboard as your part.

Make up new songs and innovate;
It's feasting time, so celebrate!
He's just, He's good: such royalty!
He's faithful, true: such loyalty!

The heavens came at His command;
That's why they're here; that's how they stand.
The oceans, seas with waves so steep
Lie undisturbed in fathomless deep.

O fear, O earth, Eternal's law,
And to His person bow in awe.
Here's why: He spoke and made our world.
At His command, the earth unfurled.

The pagan's purpose God upsets;
The nations stagger, worry, and fret.
But His eternal purpose stands;
From age to age, He works His plans.

A nation's glad with Christ enthroned;
He calls that joyful crowd His own!

He sees all men from heaven's hall:
Each thought, each deed; He sees them all.

He made each one, each human heart.
He knows His plans; He chose our part.

Not might, nor men protect a king.
The warrior's skill: a futile thing.
A tank, a jet, a bomb: false hope.
To trust in strength: a slippery slope.

God guards the ones who trust in Him;
He rules by steadfast love, not whim.
To famine or death, we will not yield,
For God is both our help and shield.

Our hearts rejoice in Him foremost;
We trust His name; in Him we boast.
Yes, we have hoped in You, our King.
Your faithful love is why we sing.

Psalm 34

HOW GOOD! HOW TRUE!

In every single moment
Of every single day
    I will bless the Lord.
My soul will sing its song of praise;
The humble ones will hear
    Rejoicing in the Lord.

And every single word I say
In every single chat
    Will be infused with praise.
O magnify the Lord with me
Exalt His name as one.
    How good! How true His ways!

I sought the Lord; He heard me.
He set me free from fears.
    How good! How true His ways!
I cried to God; He answered.
He saved me through my tears.
    How good! How true His ways!

We set our eyes on Jesus;
Our faces have no shame.
    We radiate His light.
The angel of the Lord is near
The ones who reverence God.
    He rescues in the night.

So try the way of Jesus Christ;
Surprises lie in store.
    Come learn at Jesus' feet.
Show reverence as you trust in Him;
For when you seek His way,
    He'll make your life complete.

Come, children, listen to my words;
I'll teach you how to live
    With days both good and long.
Your tongue refrain from spiteful spate,

Your lips from speaking lies.
      Do good; avoid the wrong.

The eyes of God are watching all
And open are His ears
      For those in tune with Him.
The face of God is hardening fast
To cut off evil men,
      To make their memories dim.

O seek the Lord; He'll hear your voice;
He'll hear you when you call
      And take away your tears.
He's near the ones with broken hearts,
He's near you when you're crushed.
      He'll chase away your fears.

When pain is piled on problems
For those who seek the Lord,
      He will set them free.
When pain is piled on problems
For those who hate the truth,
      They're doomed to agony.

O seek the Lord; He'll hear your voice;
Commit to serve Him well
      And walk in all His ways.
Then doom will never cross your path,
Nor catch you from behind.
      Instead you'll sing His praise.

Psalm 35

RIGHT THE WRONGS

O Great Eternal Warrior,
Fight with those who fight with me
And strike at those who strike at me
With shield and spear and axe.
O Great Eternal Champion,
Chase the ones pursuing me.
"I am your Champion!" say to me,
And counter their attacks.

Of those who seek my life:
Dishonor them and shame them all,
Cause them to stumble and to fall;
Because they seek my harm.
Send angels to pursue them;
May they slide on slippery slope,
Flailing, floundering as they grope,
Eyes aghast with wild alarm.

Of one who sets a trap:
Without a cause he waits for me,
With net and pit he schemes for me;
O boomerang his plans.
He'll reap what he has sown.
He'll trip his own destroying snares;
Destruction nets him unawares;
In his own pit he lands.

Rejoice, my soul, in Christ!
Who saves the weak from stronger powers,
And rescues man from his devourers.
He brings a brighter morn!
False accusers rise;
And charging me with evil greed,
Repaying evil for good deeds,
I'm left alone, forlorn.

I help them in their pain.
I fast, I pray, become downcast
Until their pain is gone at last;
I dress myself in black.
But when I am in pain,
They mock with cruel, cutting phrase;
They rail, revile, and rant with rage.
They're always on attack.

How long will You just watch?
Lord, save me from their loathsome lies,
From human lions who brutalize;
Let not my foes rejoice.
No words of peace are theirs.
Let not my haters wink and sneer;
Let them not shout and mock and jeer
Nor boast with taunting voice.

I will give thanks to You!
Eternal Warrior, You see all;
You rouse yourself, You hear my call;
You are not far away.
O God, defend my cause!

Disgrace the ones who seek my harm;
Dishonor those who cause alarm;
Bring on their judgment day.

And I will shout with joy;
For when You've righted all the wrongs,
Your people will burst forth in songs;
And joy will fill our days.
We all will sing this tune:
"The Lord be magnified and blest
Because at last He grants us rest."
Our tongues will trill Your praise!

Psalm 36

CONTINUE YOUR LOVE

An ungodly man with ungodly heart
Is led by ungodly whims.
When people discover his evil intent,
It only makes him more content
In the sewer where he swims.

The words of his mouth are words of deceit
And words that are mischief-born.
He despises the good, ignores the wise;
No fear of God is in his eyes;
His heart is filled with scorn.

The height of heaven, the height of Your love,
O God, Most Great, Most High!
The endless skies, Your loyalty's length;
The mountain's stone, Your justice's strength.
Beneath Your watching eye.

You guide and provide for us as we live,
Your judgments, ocean-deep.
We shelter beneath Your covering wing.
How caring Your love, O glorious King!
Protecting as we sleep.

Your house has food for discerning tastes;
We drink with great delight!
Your living fount flows from Your throne!
We live for You, for Your pleasure alone;
Our souls are full and bright.

Continue Your love to those who love You;
Be just to those who love right.
Let no ungodly leader rule;
Let each one fall who plays the fool.
Lord, lead us by Your light.

Psalm 37

GODLESS OR GOOD

Fear not the evildoers nor those who break the law;
For soon like grass they'll wilt and fade;
They'll wither like the sun-scorched blade.

Trust in the Lord Eternal; live well in His domain.
Make Jesus Christ your soul's delight;
He is the whole of good and right.

Keep nothing back from Jesus; but walk in His great
light.
He'll do whatever must be done
Your heart-deep quests at last be won.

Bring questions to the Master, like "Why do wicked rule,
Who aim to slay the upright man
While carrying out an evil plan?"

All frets end up in evil; so drop your senseless rage;
For godless men will meet their ends,
Their wealth for those whom God befriends.

The wicked grind their teeth while plotting against the
good.
God is amused at evil's jeer;
He knows their doom is drawing near.

Godless men draw swords; the Eternal grabs the hilt.
They bend their bows intent to harm;
God snaps their bows and breaks their arms.

Good men may have little; that's better than stolen
wealth.
What good men own, the Lord will guard,
Protecting him when times are hard.

The godless pass away; their families have to beg!
A fool like smoke is blown away,
Like fuel that's burned in just one day.

The good man gives and gives; the godless won't pay
debts.
Bless the Lord and own the land.
Curse the Lord--nowhere to stand.

Live your life for Christ; He makes your footing sure.
Though you may trip, you won't stay down;
You'll bounce back up, a strong rebound.

Once young, now I am old--the good man's never lost;
For he has stores from which he gives;
His offspring also generously lives.

Shun evil and do good, and trust the God of truth
Will give you life within His land
And not forsake His faithful band.

The lawless are destroyed; their godless families
doomed.

The good inherit grounds and deed,
And live forever cheered and freed.

The good man's talk is true; he speaks with wisdom words.
Eternal law is in his soul;
His steps stay pointed toward that goal.

The godless spies on good, and always digs for dirt.
The good goes free on the final day;
For the righteous God has final say.

Keep waiting for the Lord; the godless pass away.
The Lord will save you from his hand;
He'll see that you possess the land.

Like a towering redwood, there ruled an evil man.
When I returned, he wasn't found--
Not even his stump left in the ground.

A good man's worth observing, for the future belongs to him.
Transgressors run headlong to doom;
Their future lies in a stone-cold tomb.

The good man's help is God; when trouble comes, he knows
Rescue, relief with God reside.
So find the man who takes God's side.

Psalm 38

A GOOD MAN'S GUILT

Punish me not in wrath;
Punish me not in rage.
I'm starting to do the math;
My sin is paying its wage.

You've crushed me to the ground;
I am numb and badly bruised.
My body no longer is sound;
I mourn as one abused.

My bones are brittle as sticks;
My teeth a painful clench.
My sin has made me sick,
My body an odorous stench.

You know my heart's desire;
You've heard my longing sighs.
My life has lost its fire;
The light has left my eyes.

My friends avoid my path;
My family stays away.
My enemies vent their wrath--
I have no word to say.

As deaf, I do not hear.
As dumb, I do not speak.

As dead, I shed no tear.
I wait--alone and weak.

O Lord, I watch and wait.
Respond to wicked men.
I bare my guilty state;
I sorrow for my sin.

Will enemies laugh--perhaps--
And taunt me when I slip?
I'm near a full collapse;
I fear I'll lose my grip.

Many hate me strongly
For doing what I should.
Many hate me wrongly
Because I aim at good.

Forsake me not, O Master!
Be near me day by day.
Protect me from disaster;
Help me live Your way.

Psalm 39

EARTHLY GUEST

I made this claim:
I'll muzzle my mouth,
I'll zip my lips,

I'll tame my tongue
So I became
All gripped by grief
With muddled mind
And labored lung.

I prayed aloud,
"O Living Lord,
When shall I die?
My breath be gone?
A passing cloud
Is mortal man
Who works for wealth
But dies alone.

Where is my hope?
O gracious God,
It's yet in You,
Eternal, True
We mortals mope;
We wilt with guilt.
Like moths in fire,
Bid life adieu.

I'll never win,
For life's too short;
And breath is gone
In just a day
Save me from sin,
From taunts profane;
Remove your plague;
I waste away.

Eternal Crown,
This earthly guest
Cries out to You
My tears to dry
Avert Your frown,
And show Your smile
That I may rest
Before I die.

Psalm 40

KNOWING HE WOULD HELP

I waited, I looked for Jesus
Knowing He would help.
He turned to me, He heard my cry,
My whispering whine, my yelp.

My life was stuck, my progress none,
My forward motion nil.
He pulled me from a quicksand bog
And set me on a hill.

Many will see and reverence God,
For He has rescued me;
I'll sing a song of heart-felt praise,
Of joy that's strong and free.

The world's "sure thing" is a shifting thing
That worships fancy whim.

Surrender all to Jesus Christ;
True fortune comes from Him.

God-thoughts, God-deeds abound on earth
Too numerous to count.
None can compare, no words declare
This everflowing fount.

Sacrifice You've not required,
Instead You tune my ear
To You to do Your will, O Christ,
Each day, each month, each year.

I spoke Your righteous truth aloud.
I've not restrained my tongue;
For righteous truth must not be hid,
But written, spoken, sung.

Compassion You will not withhold;
Your steadfast love I see.
When evils grow and sin abounds,
My courage seems to flee.

Be pleased, O Lord, to send me help;
O hurry to my side!
And shame the ones who seek my life;
Destroy them in their pride.

Let all who seek Your face rejoice.
Let those who love you say,
"The Lord is great! The Lord is good!"
So come! Do not delay!

Psalm 41

IN YOUR HANDS

When trouble comes, do you want to be free?
When danger comes, can you escape alive?
Do you want to be blessed and live without fear?
Do you want to be healthy and vigorously thrive?
      Then help the ones who have no friend.

Be gracious, O Lord, for I've sinned against You,
And my enemies speak of my death and doom.
They all hang around to discover my flaws,
And their goal is to send me straight to the tomb.
      Even worse--I'm betrayed by a trusted friend.

It is You, O Lord, who will raise me up,
Frustrating all my enemies' plans.
By this I know that You are pleased,
You hold me ever in Your hands.
      Be blessed, O Lord, forever! Amen!

Psalm 42

DISTURBED SOUL

As the stag lifts his nose for the scent of the stream,
So my soul seeks a hint that You're here, that You're
near.

And this goal of my soul is Your presence supreme
In each sigh, in each breath, in each pulse, in each tear.

I am taunted by questions: "Where's God? Where's the
end?"
I once led the crowd to give thanks and rejoice.
I am haunted by memories of how things had been:
So eager my steps, full-throated my voice.

Now my soul is disturbed--
Why am I in despair?
I will yet hope in God;
He will answer my prayer.

Lord, my soul has lost hope; I remember the past--
How You helped in the valleys, the tall mountain's
heights.
I am overwhelmed daily; things happen so fast.
Show Your love in the mornings and songs in the nights.

I will ask of the Lord, "Why did You let me down?"
I am strongly oppressed by the fiends all around.
Their words are like jaws that are crushing my bones.
"Where is God?" they all taunt. "Has He left you alone?"

Now my soul is disturbed--
Why am I in such dread?
I will yet hope in God;
He will lift up my head!

Psalm 43

DOES GOD WITHDRAW?

Deceitful, unjust and wicked crowds
Seem stronger every day.

Take up my cause.

Depression, oppression--I'm a sad expression
Of the truth, the life, the way.

Does God withdraw?

O send Your light and truth to me
And lead me to Your place,

Your holy hill.

My greatest joy, my true delight:
To see You face to face--

My greatest thrill.

But now I'm disturbed!
Why am I in such dread?
I will yet hope in God
Who will lift up my head.

$Psalm$ 44

SAVE US NOW

We have heard with our ears how in ancient years--
Yes, our fathers have told us and the stories still hold
us--
That God cleared the land by His own sovereign hand.
The enemies were shattered and the peoples were scat-
tered.
By Your favoring smile, we won every square mile.
O our fathers knew well--and they still love to tell--
It was not by their sword, but the arm of the Lord,
And Your awesome right hand and Your mighty com-
mand.

Through You we can win, overcome evil men.
Not by sword, not by bow will we conquer the foe,
Cast aside evil powers, make the victory ours.
But of You uppermost we will sing, we will boast!

Yet You've cast us aside; You don't fight on our side.
We're the ones who retreat while our foes eat our meat.
We're like sheep to be eaten, straying dogs to be beaten.
You have sold us like dirt, like a flea market skirt.
Now that You've cast us off, all our neighbors just scoff
And laughingly poke; we're the butt of the joke.
All day long I face shame; 'Laughingstock' is my name.
Mockers come every day; I hear all that they say.

Yet we still bow to You, hold Your covenant true.

We haven't turned back; our steps are on track.
Yet life is severe; death's shadow hangs near.
If we'd forgotten Your name or served idols of shame,
Would You not know our sin? For You see deep within.

For Your sake--while You sleep, we are slaughtered like
sheep.
Rise and help us today! Do not cast us away.
You are hiding Your face; we are losing our place.
We have fallen face-down in the dust on the ground.
Rise and help us somehow; for love's sake, save us now!

Psalm 45

ROYAL REIGN

My heart is full to overflowing
To honor the King in His coming and going;
My tongue like a pen poetically poised
To honor the One that God enjoys.

More handsome than the sons of men,
Your words of grace surpassing all.
Hook on Your sword, strap on Your shield.
The world itself--Your regal hall.

Ride in majesty! Ride in victory!
Ride for truth, for order, for right.
Penetrate darkness; go straight for hearts;
Defeat Your foes with arrows of light.

Your throne is fixed, forever fixed.
Your judgments wise, wonderfully wise.
Your Father, God, has raised You up,
Exalted in joy in everyone's eyes.

Your robes are scented with fragrant spice.
Songs surround You, beautifully bold.
Noble are those who attend Your way;
Your queen beside You dressed in gold.

O bride of the King, live for Him alone;
Lay down your past and your former home;
Your beauty exclusively for the King,
Yield yourself in everything.

The distant merchant will send a gift,
The wealthy jostle to see her face--
The bride adorned in dazzling white
With brilliant gold-embroidered lace.

And down the aisle, she'll be enchanting;
Attending maids enhance the scene.
Then on with songs and joyful dancing;
And on to rule as King and Queen!

The focus will change from past to future;
Your sons in wisdom follow Your ways.
Your name extolled for generations;
Your subjects grateful all their days.

Psalm 46

PROTECTOR

God is our protection,
Our strength--its very source.
He is with us in our struggles,
When they come with raging force.

The earth--that we count stable--
Sometimes goes through massive change;
And its shifting causes oceans
To devour a mountain range.

The God of heaven's armies
Drives out fear when He is near.
Through earth-quakings, seawave-breakings,
If we call, He still can hear.

His river flows with gladness
Bringing life to you and me,
For His Spirit lives within us,
Keeps us calm when others flee.

God our peace within us;
God outside us--He's our aid.
Though nations rage and kingdoms totter,
He controls this world He made.

Look! God is in action,
For He baffles armies grand,

Breaks the strength of mighty warriors,
Takes their weapons from their hands.

Be still, my soul, and trust Him.
He's exalted over men.
He alone, the Lord of Armies,
Will protect us yet again.

Psalm 47

PRAISE TO THE KING

Everybody! Shout out!
Give standing ovations,
Raise voices of joy
To the King of all nations.

He lifts us to lead;
We are raised to reign,
And because of His love,
An inheritance gain.

He ascends to His throne
Amid trumpet and shout!
O sing songs of praise,
His subjects devout.

Sing your best, play with skill;
He is King of all earth!

Let your praises describe
His infinite worth.

Let all leaders draw near,
Yield to Him everything.
Any safety on earth
Is a boon from the King!

Psalm 48

GOD-BUILT COMMUNITY

The Lord is great! Let His praise abound
From His people as one on His holy ground.
When godly ones rule, the earth sings a song;
God governs through them and the nation is strong.

The kings of the earth are befuddled, amazed,
Even panicked to see the results of God's ways.
The forces of nature flow from His reserve,
Submit to His will, His purposes serve.

Now we see with our eye what we heard with our ear:
How God makes us strong, stabilizes our sphere.
We have thought of Your love so steadfast and strong
And we join with Your throng in a global praise-song.

Our relationships thrive for Your hand is upon us;
Your wisdom-ways work and Your joy is a bonus.
Travel the world and consider God's people,
Comprising His building, his walls, and His steeple.

Consider their hearts, how they generously give;
And train up your youth to adopt how they live.
For Jesus is God; He has overcome death!
His Spirit will guide you until your last breath.

Psalm 49

POMPOUS MAN

Everybody! Listen up!
Every solitary soul,
Low and high, rich and poor,
Listen up! Listen up!

I am speaking wisdom words:
Meditations from my heart,
Proverb truths, probing questions.
Wisdom words; wisdom words.

Trouble comes; I'll not fear,
Although evil men surround,
Trusting riches, boasting wealth.
I'll not fear; I'll not fear.

Life on sale? Not by man!
Can money resurrect the dead?
Prevent death? Restore the breath?
Not by man! Not by man!

We must see that all men die.
All their wealth they leave to others.
Dunce or wit, stupid, wise--
All men die; all men die.

He thinks he counts--Pompous man!
He thinks he'll leave a mark enduring,
A lasting name, or home, or land.
Pompous man! Pompous man!

Foolish man, this is your path
And the path of those who follow:
Death, the grave, darkness, hell--
This is your path; this is your path.

But here's a mystery: God can do it!
Snatch your soul from evil's grasp:
From death, the grave, darkness, hell.
God can do it. God can do it.

When man ascends, do not fear.
When glory in his house increases,
He'll die, he'll pass, his glory vanish.
Do not fear; do not fear.

O pompous man, understand.
You love the accolades of others;
All will pass; but God will last.
Understand . . . Understand.

Psalm 50

PLAINLY SPEAKING

God the mighty Lord has spoken: spoken truth to all the
world.
His majestic glory shining, shining as the priceless pearl.
Heaven and earth are called to witness, witness judg-
ment of mankind.
Gather the godly for His blessing, blessing evil men can't
find.

God is calling to the people, people who have shut their
ears.
God their Source is always wooing, wooing them
throughout the years.
People bring their sacrifices, sacrifices to appease.
But God who owns it all is wary, wary of half-hearted
pleas.

Never hungry, He has no need, need of meat or drink or
loan.
Within Himself, He is sufficient, sufficient in Himself
alone.
Honor God with your thanksgiving, giving thanks and
vowing true.
In the day of trouble calling, calling Him to rescue you.

To the wicked God is saying, saying, "Why, oh, why do
you
Twist the covenant I've offered, offered--but you mis-

construe?
You hate my ways as 'too restricting', restricting rules to be ignored.
The path of thieves, adulterers choosing, choosing paths that I abhor.

"Your lips are loose, your words are weaving, weaving wicked schemes and plots.
Your mother's son you sit and slander, slander brother with your rot.
You do these things, and I've kept silence--silence you misunderstand,
Thinking I am just like you are. You are ripe for reprimand!

"I will put it to you plainly. Plainly hear it, and you'll gasp.
Consider this: you have no safety. Safety has escaped your grasp.
Ignore Me and your life is shambles--shambles, shakings, disarray.
Instead, give thanks. If this you give me--give me thanks, I'll lead your way."

Psalm 51

CONFESSION

Grant grace, O God,
Grant mercy and love.
And in Your great compassion
Blot out all my sin.
Wash me, O God,
Cleanse me all through.
For in my great transgression,
I'm stained without, within.

I know my sin,
I see it now.
I've made myself an idol--
I've broken faith with You.
Brought forth in sin,
Conceived in sin,
I'm now before Your judgment;
Your verdict will be true.

You want Your truth
To pierce my core;
And there to plant Your spirit
To purify my soul.
Wash me throughout,
As white as snow.
Then tune my heart to gladness--
Make me new and whole.

Create in me
A heart that's clean,
A spirit that is focused;
Don't cast me far away.
Do not withdraw
Your Spirit's strength.
Encourage me with kindness;
Renew my heart today.

Then I will teach
Self-serving men
To come back home to You
And learn Your faithful ways.
I self-destruct;
Free me from self.
I'll sing of God the Faithful,
My tongue aflame with praise!

A sacrifice
Will not suffice.
You are not pleased with offerings.
Your grace cannot be sold.
A humble heart,
A searching soul--
In these You find delight,
For these are heaven's gold.

Do good to us;
Build up, build up.
And we will bring thanksgiving:
Your sacrifice of choice.
A sign of peace:

Whole--hearted gifts
Of gratitude and praises.
Once more we will rejoice.

Psalm 52

GOD-TRUST

You boast and You brag, O man of power,
Oppress good folks each day, each hour.
Your tongue's so sharp, it isn't felt
When life is sliced away, death dealt.
You love your lies and wrong esteem;
You relish the words that hide your scheme.

But God will come and pull you down,
Dislodge you from your evil town.
He'll snatch you up right out of your boots;
He'll pull you up branch, trunk, and roots.

God-trusting men will relish relief
At the end of the tyrant who caused their grief,
Who had trusted wealth and all he'd acquired
To prolong the power he'd wrongly desired.

But I am alive like a green olive tree,
And I thrive in the house of the God who loves me.
I rely on His kindness, depend on His grace.
Forever He rules from His unshaken place.

I will praise You for all that You do, all You've done!
I'll declare how You love us and sent us Your Son.
I'll join with the God-trusting women and men
Who rely on Your just-love again and again.

Psalm 53

FUTURE FEAR?

A man is a fool saying, "There's no God."
His whole life askew, nothing quite right.
God looks from heaven, surveys mankind
To find one with sense, walking in light.

But all are corrupted, distracted and lost.
Not one hits center; no, not even one!
They've lived for themselves; regret is their lot;
Having trampled on others, ignoring God's Son.

Fear is their future, for God will arrive,
Scatter their bones and leave them in shame.
Salvation is coming to people of praise;
When God sets them free, they'll rejoice in His name.

Psalm 54

CONFIDENCE

Save me, O God, in this hour,
And uphold me now by Your power.
O Lord, hear my cries,
Take note of my sighs.
Deliver from those who devour.

You are the One who sustains,
Who strengthens when everything pains.
You deliver from woes.
You defeat all my foes.
I'm singing thanksgiving refrains.

Psalm 55

BETRAYAL

Listen, O God; hear me, O God!
Attend me and answer my bitter protest.
My foe is afoot, and bullies about;
I fear my heart's throbbing may burst in my chest.

Godless men shout and threaten to harm,
Attacking with fury, they boast and they gloat.
Horror now holds me; terror enfolds me;
Trembling and anguish have throttled my throat.

If I had wings like the wings of a dove,
I'd fly far away, find shelter above.
Above all the fury, confusion, and storm;
I'd rest in a refuge where "safe" is the norm.

Confuse them, O Lord; divide them, O Lord;
For violence and strife run rife through the streets.
In day they are bold; at night blood-cold
With iniquity, mischiefs, murders, deceits.

Destruction is rampant; oppression is fierce;
But the heart-breaking fact that is shaking my soul:
My companion, my friend, my brother, my kin
Has betrayed all of us and is seizing control!

May Death ring his bell; let him slide down to hell;
Let him scream and protest as he enters its gate.
He was smooth when he talked; he was soft in his
words;
But his thoughts were to harm, and his heart harbored
hate.

As for me I will call for the help of the Lord
Evening and morning and noon, every day.
He will hear all my moanings, my sighings, my groanings
And at the right moment set free from this fray.

Take the weight of the world and give Him your burden;
He'll surely sustain you and cause you to stand.

He will deal with the wicked; their lives will be short-
ened,
If you trust in Him and His Almighty Hand.

Psalm 56

OVERCOMING FEAR OF MAN

Take my side, O God, against ungodly men;
They kick, they stomp, they trample.
Not a day goes by that I'm not in a fight--
And this is just a sample.

But when I'm afraid,
I trust in You.
Your word I praise,
And trust in You.
I shall not fear
What man can do.

Throughout the day, they distort my words.
They watch, they lurk, they attack.
They choose the moment to take my life;
O Lord, turn their wickedness back.

You've taken account of my muddled response:
My tears, my fear, my ache.
When I call on You, turn the prowlers away;
Restore what they've tried to take.

Now this I know:
That God is true.
His word I praise;
His word is true.
I shall not fear
What man can do.

I belong to You; I am full of thanks.
You deliver, You act, You embrace.
Now my steps are sure, for I walk with You
And I live in the glow of Your grace.

Psalm 57

AWAKE, MY PRAISE

Bend down, O Lord; bend down to me.
My soul finds rest in You.
I rest, O God, I rest in Your shade
As destruction passes through.

I cry, O God, I cry to You
To save from those who abuse.
You act, O God, on my behalf
With steadfast love and truth.

I live, O Lord, I live among lions,
My soul among men of power.
Their teeth, O Lord, their teeth like swords,
With razor's edge to devour.

A trap, O Lord, a trap for me!
A hole dug just my fit.
Hallelu, O Lord, Hallelu, Hallelu!
They're caught in their own dark pit.

Be exalted, O God, be exalted high,
Your glory beyond all earth.
I will sing, O Lord, I will sing and praise
Your splendid, infinite worth.

Awake, my praise. Awake harp and lyre;
Awaken the light of the dawn.
Give thanks to the Lord, with others give thanks.
Make praises go on and on.

How great your truth. How great to the clouds,
And Your love beyond highest height.
Be exalted, O God, be exalted high,
And fill the earth with light!

Psalm 58

HOPE FOR JUSTICE

Do men of power decree what is best?
Are their judgments helpful to all the rest?
No, they serve themselves in what they decide,
And they rationalize violence because of their pride.

There are those from the womb who are wickedly turned;
Their language is lies, and the truth they spurn.
Like venomous vipers that can't be charmed,
They release their poisons, not caring what's harmed.

God, shatter their teeth and break off their fangs.
May their arrows be headless, their bows empty twangs.
Like salted slugs, may they all melt away;
May their plans never hatch; may they never see day.

The righteous rejoice when God's vengeance appears,
And the blood of the wicked repays all their tears.
The righteous will say, "Yes, there is a reward!
There is justice on earth when the judge is the Lord."

Psalm 59

RESILIENT SONG

Rescue me, God, from all my foes.
Protect me from the evil flood,
From men who thirst for evil deeds;
Yes, save me from these men of blood.

A lurking gang, they want my life;
They shadow my steps for an opportune time.
O Lord of armies, spare them not;
I've done no wrong, committed no crime.

With insolent insults on their lips,
Like a pack of snarling dogs they prowl.
They report to none, fear no rebuke,
And scare the weak with chilling howl.

O Eternal God, You laugh at them.
You mark their bluster and their pride.
You are my Strength, I sing Your song.
With You my soul is fortified.

In Your strong love You stand with me;
We triumph over the enemy-force,
Dispense them, scatter them, bring them down,
And leave a warning for future course.

Each word they utter is a sin.
With boasts, they build a proud facade.
Destroy them 'til they cease to be,
'Til earth awakes to the rule of God.

With insolent insults on their lips,
Like a pack of snarling dogs they prowl.
They roam in search of innocent prey,
And if they miss it, grumble and growl.

I sing a tune of Your great love,
Of You my Strength, my Refuge-strong.
Of danger gone, of strength renewed;
For You, Eternal, are my song.

Psalm 60

WHO ELSE, BUT YOU?

We feel discarded, crushed in anger!
God, restore our strength.
You've taken, shaken, scattered and shattered;
Rebuked our sin at length.

When trials came, we failed the test
And lost our lofty seat.
Though You gave us a flag to fly,
We fled in full retreat.

We are Your children, Yours by birth;
And so we used Your name.
Cocksure, we marched to fight the foe--
You left us to our shame.

We need You here in battle gear!
Show up! Our wins will grow.
Man-help is never quite enough;
But You defeat our foe.

Announce Your plans with joyful tone,
Full-dressed in glorious light.
With gift-wrapped spoils from conquered towns,
We'll party through the night.

"For Gilead's mine, Manasseh's mine,
Ephraim is my hat.

Judah's a sign of how I rule:
What do you think of that?

Moab's a bowl to wash my hands,
Edom, a rest for My feet.
And Palestine a place of peace,
Where justice and love will meet."

Who leads us to the battle's roar?
Who rides with unsheathed sword?
Who gives us courage in our hearts?
Who else, but You, O Lord?

Psalm 61

YOUR GUEST

Hear my cry, O hear my prayer.
You seem far away as I'm trying to cope:
My troubles confuse; please show me a way.
You are my help, my only hope.

To be Your guest, O God, to rest
Within the safety of Your halls
And to receive this one request:
To share with those who hear Your call.

The King lives on from age to age;
He lives with You forevermore,
Upheld by truth and steadfast love.

I'll sing Your praise forevermore;
My days are Yours forevermore.

Psalm 62

MY QUIET COMMITMENT

I quietly commit myself to God,
For He alone makes me endure:
Foundation, walls, my place of trust.
When shaking comes, I am secure.

A gang, they come to pull me down,
Destroy my place, bring death to all.
They treat me like a shaky fence,
An unhinged door, a tottering wall.

They scheme and plot to undermine,
Delight in their deceptive "smarts."
Though flattery flows from friendly lips,
They come with curses in their hearts.

I quietly commit myself to God,
For He alone makes me endure:
Foundation, walls, my place of trust.
When shaking comes, I am secure.

My help, my hope are found in God.
His granite-strength will ever stand.

Live bold with Him your place of trust:
Your cares, your plans within His hand.

For man's a wisp, a brief mirage;
He has no weight on eternal scales.
Man's power is "smoke-and-mirror" mush.
In the test of time, it always fails.

One--God says it. Two--I hear it:
All power truly is the Lord's;
And in His rule of righteous love,
Each person gets his just reward.

I quietly commit myself to God,
For He alone makes me endure:
Foundation, walls, my place of trust.
When shaking comes, I am secure.

Psalm 63

MY LIPS WILL SING

You are my God,
I yearn for You.
Body and soul,
I thirst for You.
Like land without water,
Weary and dry,
I seek You, God;
I thirst for You.

You're the Holy Place!
In Your presence I see
Visions of power,
Majestic grace.
While I yet live,
I will bless Your name.
Lifting my hands,
To majestic grace.

Your love is more
Than life to me.
My mouth will praise,
My lips will sing.
I'm satisfied,
I offer praise--
With songs of mirth,
My lips will sing.

When I lie down,
I think of You.
Remembering You
In dark of night.
My soul grasps You;
Your grip holds me.
I sing Your praise
In dark of night.

Some seek my death,
Yet they will die,
Run through by sword,
While men rejoice.
When evil mouths

Are gagged like that,
The leaders laugh
And men rejoice.

Psalm 64

GOD'S WISE VENGEANCE

Hear me, O God; I whine in my room.
I whimper in fear of the Day of Doom.
Conspirators search, they've perfected their arts;
Their words are like weapons, like poisoned darts.

Concealing their actions with words of charm,
Their evil inventions multiply harm.
They blackmail, extort, concealing their crime;
So sure they are safe, they smirk all the time.

Omniscient God steps in to avenge;
And the ones who were smug now cower and cringe.
They double in pain, bewildered, deposed;
For everyone sees their schemings exposed.

Men will declare the work of the Lord,
Noting His truth, respecting His sword.
Men who love right find cheer in God's choice;
And the man who trusts Him will sing and rejoice.

Psalm 65

JOY IN THE EARTH

Silence and sound
Abound with praise
For the Creator
From whom all things flow.
Men in their smallness
Bring prayer to You.
God of compassion,
Forgiveness bestow.

Happy and blest,
We're guests in Your courts.
The God who invites us
To come and draw near
Fills us all up
With the cup of thanksgiving--
God of abundance,
Of joy and of cheer.

Awesome, amazing,
How dazzling Your deeds,
God of Creation
Who does all things well.
All of the worth
Of the earth and the seas--
God's handiwork
Cannot be excelled.

In might You made mountains
Stand firm and stand fixed,
And the tumults of nations
And oceans to cease.
In Your joy You made dawn
And dusk to give shout,
So the ends of the earth
Rejoice in Your peace.

You visit the earth;
The earth resounds.
You enrich the earth--
New life abounds.
You prepare the earth--
You multiply grain.
You water its furrows
With softening rain.
You bless its growth
From county to county.
You crown the year
With beauteous bounty.
Wherever You walk
New things come alive.
The wilderness deserts
Revive and thrive.
The hills are rejoicing,
The meadows have mirth,
The valleys are singing;
There's joy in the earth!

Psalm 66

MY NEED: GOD'S STRENGTH

Everyone in all the earth,
Shout to God with joy!
Sing the glory of His name,
Praise Him and increase His fame.
Shout to God with joy!

How awesome are Your works, O God!
How awesome is Your power!
Enemies fear Your judgment day;
They all pretend that they'll obey.
How awesome is Your power!

Come and see the works of God;
Come and sing His praise.
All the earth will worship Him,
Awesome in His deeds toward men.
Come and sing His praise!

With walls of water on each side,
They walked across dry land.
Who has ever heard of such?
The sea stood up at His great touch!
They walked across dry land.

Forever by His might He rules;
Let us rejoice in Him.
As nations bloom, as nations flower,

Let not rebellious men gain power.
Let us rejoice in Him.

O every people, bless our God
And sound His praise abroad.
He keeps us safe in all of life
And strengthens us in every strife.
O sound His praise abroad.

You test us and You try us, Lord,
Refining us by fire.
You bring us to a place of lack;
You place a burden on our backs,
Refining us by fire.

I yield my body to Your will;
I'm paying what I vowed.
When I was in distress, O Lord,
I promised I would serve You, Lord.
I'm paying what I vowed.

God brought me to a plenteous place.
I'll tell of what He's done.
I cried to Him when things went south.
I eked out praises from my mouth.
I'll tell of what He's done.

He doesn't hear the wicked's word;
He heard my heartfelt prayer.
When I was in my deepest need
His love--so loyal--set me free.
He heard my heart-felt prayer.

Psalm 67

LET NATIONS SEE

Smile on us, Lord,
And show Your face;
Make plain your purpose to men.
The world will see
Your saving grace,
And praise again and again.

The nations sing
And joyfully praise,
So glad You rule the earth.
They all will sing,
They all will raise
Their voices for Your worth.

The lands produce
That You have blessed
With rivers from Your throne.
Let all men shout,
Their praise expressed,
"Glory to God alone!"

Psalm 68

WHEN GOD RULES

When God arises,
Enemies flee;
Like a puff of smoke,
Like melting wax,
They're gone! They're gone!

Then good men laugh
And celebrate big.
They clap their hands;
They dance a jig.
They sing; they sing.

God is Father
Of an orphaned child,
A help to widows
Who've been reviled--
Alone. Alone.

God makes a place
For lonely souls;
And debtors turn
When God controls.
Fools crave. Fools crave.

God leads us forth;
The mountains quake;
God leads our march;

The heavens shake.
Great God! Great God!

The rains poured down;
The land revived.
God favored us--
And then we thrived.
He's good! He's good!

The Lord commands
And women praise.
They share the spoils
Of winning ways.
Kings flee! Kings flee!

Like the wings of a dove
That shimmer with snow,
The women wear silver
And gold from the foe.
They dance, they dance.

God chose a mount--
Sinai's peak.
His presence there
Made it unique.
God spoke; God spoke.

He's in the midst
Of His loyal hosts.
Their hearts are His
To the uttermost.
They bow. They bow.

Our saving God
Sets free our souls
And daily bears
Our heavy loads.
Give thanks! Give thanks!

Our foes will hear
God's gavel rap;
Their blood when spilled,
The dogs will lap.
Destroyed. Destroyed.

Your people marched
In Your parade.
The singers sang;
The players played
In praise, in praise.

The maidens beat
Their tambourines,
And all the people
Joined the scene.
Bless God! Bless God!

God puts His strength
Into your staff
And acts today
In your behalf.
Be strong. Be strong.

All kings will bring
Their gifts to You
And gladly make
Their vows anew!
They yield. They yield.

As beasts stampede
What men adore,
God scatters those
Who live for war.
Dispersed. Dispersed.

Foreign nations
Scrape and bow,
Submitting power,
Making vows,
They pledge. They pledge.

O earthly kingdoms,
Sing His praise.
Of God the Highest,
Be amazed.
Exalt! Exalt!

Ascribe to Him--
Go to great lengths--
Ascribe to Him
All might, all strength.
Exult! Exult!

O Awesome God,
From Your own place,

Grant us new strength,
Grant us Your grace.
Be blessed! Be blessed!

$\mathcal{P}$salm 69

PRAYER FOR RESCUE

God save me! I'm stuck;
I fear I will drown.
There's a mighty flood flowing,
And I'm going down.
My voice is a rasp;
My eyes are all red;
My enemies more
Than the hairs on my head.
Those who were friends
Now turn to attack.
What I never took--
Must I somehow pay back?

You know all my wrongs;
My follies You see.
May those who fear You
Never be shamed by me.
Though I've been estranged
From my own brother's face,
They'll not be dishonored
Who seek Your embrace,

My zeal for You,
My life approach,
My heart for You,
All bring reproach.
I fast for You;
They say I'm weak.
I dress in rags;
They call me "Freak!"
Their leaders say
I'm a public flunk.
I'm even the joke
Of the public drunk.

In steadfast love,
Lord, change their tune,
For I pray to you;
O answer me soon.

All this abuse
Puts me in fear.
Don't let me down,
Please linger near.
May evil's flood
Not swamp my soul
Nor swallow me up
In its deep, dark hole.

O, answer me now,
Good God of love,
And turn toward me
From high above.
Don't hide Your face;

I'm so distressed;
Rescue this soul
That's so oppressed.

Reproach and shame,
Dishonor, too,
Are all familiar,
Lord, to You.
I'm nauseated,
Deeply pained.
No sympathy found,
No comfort gained.

My drink is soured,
My food is drugged.
May tables be turned,
May the thieves get mugged,
And fleeing their homes
With hearts full of ache,
May they become blind,
And tremble and shake.

When You wound a man,
They all gather round,
And kick and attack
The one that is down.
Their darkness and guilt
Shut them off from the right.
O blot them from life,
Yes, keep them from light.

Meanwhile I ask,
"Set me safely on high;
I will praise and give thanks,
You alone magnify."
The "thanks" sacrifice
To God is the best.
And all men are equal
When put to that test.

Good news for the humble--
Be encouraged, all;
He tends to the needy,
Hears prisoners call.
From heaven and earth,
From oceans and skies,
Let everything praise,
Let thanks arise.
God saves; God builds;
We dwell and possess,
And loving Him, live
A life that is blessed.

Psalm 70

CONTRAST

Oh, help me, Eternal One;
Rescue me, hasten!
And those who would scoff,
Thwart them and chasten.

Those who would harm me,
Display their dishonor.
Those who would murder,
Disrupt and disgrace them.

But those who would honor You
May they be praising,
And joyous refrains
May they ever be raising.
As for me, I am weak;
God, be my strength,
My help, my deliverer;
You are amazing!

Psalm 71

HOPE KEEPS ON

You are my personal refuge, Lord;
Deliver me from blame.
O bend to me, O gracious God,
And set me free from shame.

You are my safe-house in the rock,
An ever strong defense.
You sent the word that I could live
Set free from my torments.

Rescue me from wicked men,
So cruel, cold, uncouth.
When life's a drag, inspire me on--
You've done this since my youth.

You've kept me going since my birth;
Your praise has been my song.
And many marvel at my faith;
You are my refuge strong!

When enemies plot to do me in
And think I am forsaken,
Don't leave me here, don't cast me off;
But show them they're mistaken.

Don't be distant; be my help.
'Til enemies are consumed.
Let those who plot to injure me
Be planning their own doom.

As for me, my hope keeps on;
I'll praise You more than ever.
I'll tell Your stories, sing Your glories--
Praise: my great endeavor.

I will recite Your awesome deeds
And praise Your faithful aid.
Your truth has made my life a song;
I sing Your accolades.

When I am old with graying hair,
O Lord, do not forsake.

I'll pass Your truth to younger ones
So they can come partake.

The mind of man cannot explain
The deeds that You have done.
The universe cannot contain
Your essence, Holy One.

You've made us suffer many trials,
Difficult and sore.
But You revive us from the depths
And raise us up once more.

You've added honor to our joy
And strength for every need.
I'll sing and play Your praise, O God,
For every faithful deed.

Now those who tried to do me harm
Will run away headlong.
My lips will shout; my tongue will sing;
My soul will dance along.

Psalm 72

PRAYER FOR LEADERS

Lord, give the gift of wisdom to my son,
That as he rules he may with justice lead.
And may he value people

Who are in your image made,
And honor humble men when they're in need.

May leaders everywhere become inspired
To do what's right for those they lead;
May that be their desire.

May he take the cause of those who are in pain
And see their children strengthened in their youth.
May he crush the cruel oppressor
'Til he fears the righteous reign,
And coming generations gain the truth.

May leaders everywhere become inspired
To do what's right for those they lead;
May that be their desire.

May he come like rain upon the thirsty grass,
Like showers softly soaking in the ground.
In his days may good men flourish
And may peace increase and nourish
Everyone who hears his voice and heeds the sound.

May leaders everywhere become inspired
To do what's right for those they lead;
May that be their desire.

May he rule from sea to sea and shore to shore
From the desert dust to rivers running free.
May his enemies fall down
Groveling, groping on the ground.
Every king--both east and west--come bow the knee.

May leaders everywhere become inspired
To do what's right for those they lead;
May that be their desire.

When the needy cry, he strides onto the scene;
For the helpless and afflicted he will fight.
With compassion he will save
The ones oppressors have enslaved,
For their life-blood will be precious in his sight.

May leaders everywhere become inspired
To do what's right for those they lead;
May that be their desire.

May he live and may true riches come his way,
And may others bless his name and sing his worth.
Because of him: abundant fields,
Fruit that multiplies its yields,
And like plants, his people flourish in the earth.

May leaders everywhere become inspired
To do what's right for those they lead;
May that be their desire.

May his name endure forever and increase;
Let the men of every nation find his peace.
Blessed be the God of mystery
Who reveals his might in history.
May his glory fill the earth and never cease!

Psalm 73

YOUR NEARNESS IS MY GOODNESS

God is good to the good,
But for a while I couldn't tell;
I almost slipped, I almost fell.

How I envied self-made men,
How they prospered, had no pain,
Had no troubles, only gain.

They wear pride like a jewel;
They wear violence like a coat.
How they swagger, how they gloat.

Mocking, looking down their noses,
Cursing heaven, seizing earth:
"Does God know? What is His worth?"

Then I thought, "I've been a fool;
I've kept my life from sinful stain
All in vain, all in vain."

It would just betray my children,
If I said these thoughts aloud;
Yet I thought them anyhow.

Then I saw God's view, His secret:
See the long run, and endure.
They'll soon be gone; their ruin is sure.

Evil, in a single moment,
Like a vapor dissipates--
Flees in fear, yes, abdicates.

I am dull, misunderstanding
When I'm sour, when I'm sore,
Like the beast outside the door.

Yet You're with me, yet You hold me,
Guiding me with counsel wise,
Guarding me with watchful eyes.

You alone make heaven heaven.
Without You, there's no reward.
Your nearness is my goodness, Lord.

Without God, my heart will fail;
Without God, I moan and mope;
But God is strength and God is hope.

Lord, You are my place of safety.
Lord, You are my great reward.
Your nearness is my goodness, Lord.

Psalm 74

ESTABLISH THE LIMITS

You moved off; You left us.
You kept straight ahead.
How could You just walk
And leave us for dead?

Remember Your people!
You made us Your own.
You lived here among us,
Our dwellings Your home.

Come see the disaster
And check out the mess:
Our enemies rising
And causing distress.

Like a fool with an ax
Destroying what's good
With shattering swings
On antiques of wood,
They've burned up Your house,
Defiling Your name,
Oppressing us all,
Displaying our shame.

Nothing gives hope;
No prophecy's heard.
How long will this last?

Please send us Your word.

The enemies mock,
Your name ever spurn.
Now unsheathe Your sword;
With vengeance return!

O King of the ages,
Take note of our needs--
In the midst of the earth,
Work deliverance deeds.

You divided the seas
And revealed in the deep
The sea monster's lair
And crushed him for keeps.

The landscape You changed,
Turned the deserts to seas,
Turned the seas into deserts--
Brought earth to its knees.

Yours is the day;
Yours is the night;
Yours is the sun;
Yours is the light.

Yours are the seasons,
The spring and the fall.
You establish the limits,
The boundaries for all.

113

So limit the fools
Who have tarnished Your name.
Bring an end to their reach;
Bring an end to their fame.

O guard from the beast,
And hold by Your hand.
Your covenant keep--
There's war in the land.

Return the oppressed,
Their honor restore!
The needy lift up
To praise You once more.

As the foolish men boast
In continual roar,
Arise in Your might
And settle the score.

Psalm 75

GOD'S APPOINTMENTS

Thanks, thanks, and more thanks, God!
We bring our thanks to You.
Men declare Your wondrous works,
Your name that's Faithful-True.

You said You'd pick an appointed time;
 You said You'd justly judge.
The men of earth will melt away
 But earth itself won't budge.

To boastful men, You say, "Don't boast.
 Don't strut with haughty stride."
To bossy men, You say, "Don't boss.
 Don't prattle on in pride."

Not east nor west, not north nor south
 Protect, promote, provide;
For God's the judge who raises one
 And sets the rest aside.

God has a cup of bitter wine
 Well mixed for wicked men.
And they will drink it to the dregs--
 The poison of their sin.

I'm singing praise to Jesus Christ
 Who settles every score:
The wicked evermore cast down,
 God's loyal ones restored.

Psalm 76

JUDGMENT'S DAWN

God is revealed in praise,
And those He's changed
Declare his grace.
God shows Himself in peace,
And makes our hearts
His dwelling place.

He melts the stout of heart;
And those on watch
Sink into sleep.
The bravest fail to fight,
For rider and horse
Drown in the deep.

He breaks the swords of war
And makes them dull
Within the fray.
He gleams with splendor bright
Like snow-capped peaks
At dawn of day.

God is the One to fear,
For who can stand
His angry gaze?
God's judgment sounds on high;
Earth hears and fears,
And counts her days.

God rises up to judge,
To avenge the weak
Throughout the earth.
Man's error ends in praise.
God takes man's sin--
Reveals His worth.

You made a vow to God?
Don't cast it down,
But give it wing!
Let everyone yield all
To Him who knows
Each single thing.

He breaks the heart of pride;
And kings will fear
His sovereign way.
He gleams in splendor bright
Like snow-capped peaks
At dawn of day.

Psalm 77

HONEST QUESTIONS

My spirit grows faint when God isn't near;
I cry out to Him; I know He will hear.
In trouble I seek Him, I'm doing my best.
If I could just reach Him, my soul could find rest.

I ponder this thought: "Has God become weak?"
My eyes will not shut; my lips cannot speak.
I remember the days when we sang with full hearts.
Has His love for us stopped? We seem far apart.

I remember Your deeds, Your wonders now past.
Your power gave life; Your love was steadfast.
When I think on Your works, what god is like You,
Who has shown Himself great, so faithful, so true?

The waters thrashed; the clouds gave shout;
Your lightnings flashed; and thunders roared out.
You made safe paths through mountains steep;
By chosen men, You led Your sheep.

Psalm 78

DON'T BE LIKE YOUR FATHERS

Listen, my children, and open your ears.
I will tell you a tale; to your eyes bring tears.
We have heard, we have known, for our fathers have told
Of the praises of God--His wonders of old.

He made us a witness; He gave us His law
So our fathers would teach and we could recall;
And those yet unborn will grow up and guide
Their children to trust and keep God on their side.

> Don't be like your fathers who wandered away,
> Didn't tend to their hearts and straggled astray.

Though the archers were apt, when it counted, they ran!
Rejecting God's word and His covenant plan,
They forgot what He'd done and the wonders they saw
In escaping from Egypt in shock and in awe!

God divided the sea as His people took flight
With His cloud in the day, with His fire in the night.
He made wilderness rock become fountains, it seems;
And rumbling-rock waters rushed out in a stream.

Yet they sinned, they rebelled, putting God to the test:
Could He serve them some food in this waste wilder-
ness?
They had drunk from the waters, refreshed from the
heat;
But could He give bread? And could He give meat?

> Don't be like your fathers who wandered away,
> Didn't tend to their hearts and straggled astray.

As the Lord heard their groanings, His anger arose;
For they doubted His power while His pool cooled their
toes.
Yet He opened the clouds; He unlocked heaven's doors--
They ate manna from heaven; they ate heaven's stores.

Quail flew from the south; birds came from the east;
And they fell near their tents--God provided a feast!
To prepare and to eat was the multitude's task.

So their stomachs were filled--God gave what they
asked.

God's anger was riled; and some of them died;
For they did not believe in the God who provides.
With the meat in their mouths, some choked on their
error;
And failing to thank Him, they ended in terror.

When some of them died, the others recalled
That God was their rock, so on Him they called.
But their mouths were misleading; their lips speaking
lies.
Their hearts neither steady nor covenant-wise.

> Don't be like your fathers who wandered away,
> Didn't tend to their hearts and straggled astray.

Yet God in compassion forgave them their sin.
Restraining His anger, He took them back in.
He remembered their flesh, that they were but men,
Like wind passing by, not returning again.

They often rebelled, giving God no relief,
Ever testing His patience and causing Him grief,
Forgetting God's power, His great mighty hand
That freed them from Egypt and slavery's land.

The rivers of Egypt God turned into blood;
Flies came in swarms; frogs came in floods.
Crops were laid bare by locusts and hail;
And cattle were killed by lightning-filled gale.

Anger and fury were messengers sent
To accompany death with horrid intent,
Seeking the firstborns, and taking each life,
Leaving all Egypt in grief-stricken strife.

But His chosen He led like a flock of sheep
While the army of Egypt drowned in the deep.
God guided through deserts by His holy hand
To the heights and the hilltops of His holy land.

He drove out the nations that lived in the land
And gave it to Israel to rule and command.
He divided the land, giving each clan its plot;
And within every clan, each man had his lot.

Yet they doubted, defied, disobeyed God Most High.
They fell; they were false, even failing to try.
They trusted in idols of wood and of stone.
They slandered God's ways, struck out on their own.

He was jealous for them--they despised their own
worth.
He abandoned the tent He had pitched on the earth.
The ark of His presence He allowed to be taken;
The people He loved He allowed to be shaken.

Many were captured and they became slaves;
Their warriors were speared and filled up the graves.
Girls had no weddings; their men died at war.
Priests were all murdered, their widows ignored.

Don't be like your fathers who wandered away,
Didn't tend to their hearts and straggled astray.

Then it seemed God awoke as if from a sleep.
He faced down the foes, made their widows weep.
He drove them all back 'til they turned and they ran;
And then He made Judah the prominent clan.

He made David king, who had tended the sheep,
Who had cared for the lambs, and guarded their sleep.
Now guiding the nation, protecting their lands,
He ruled like a shepherd--brave heart and skilled hands.

Psalm 79

IS YOUR ANGER NOT DONE?

O God . . .O God
O God . . . O God.

We've been invaded,
Your temple reviled.
The city's in ruins,
Our corpses defiled.
Food for the birds,
Feasts for the beasts,
Our blood has been spilled,
No tombs for deceased.

We're a reproach,
Scoffed and derided.
Is Your anger not done?
Is Your wrath not subsided?
Others around
Don't know You at all;
They don't bow the knee,
Or Your name ever call.

They razed all our houses,
Devoured our lands.
Then they mockingly ask,
"Are you still in God's hands?"
Forgive us the sins
Of our fathers before us;
Cause Your compassion
To come and restore us.

O God of our help,
We are low; we are down.
Come cancel our sins;
Deliver our town.
Why should the pagans
Doubt You are real?
Show up with vengeance;
Your power reveal!

May the one doomed to die
Be set free--hear his groan.
May the ones who abuse
Feel the wrath of Your throne.
We Your people, like sheep,

Will follow Your ways,
And to all generations
Will sing of Your praise.

Psalm 80

GRANT US YOUR FAVOR

O Leader of lambs, O Shepherd of sheep,
Come tend to Your flock, Your people to keep.
O God of great strength, O great saving Lord,
Grant us Your favor, and we'll be restored.

O Lord over angels, let anger subside.
We plead and we pray, "Come stand by our side."
O God of great strength, O great saving Lord,
Grant us Your favor, and we'll be restored.

Our bread is our pain, our drink is our tears.
We're the butt of the jokes, the object of jeers.
O God of great strength, O great saving Lord,
Grant us Your favor, and we'll be restored.

You freed us from slavery and made this land clear.
Like a vine we took root when you planted us here.
O God of great strength, O great saving Lord,
Grant us Your favor, and we'll be restored.

We spread over mountains, we covered the trees.
We reached to the River, we spread to the seas.

O God of great strength, O great saving Lord,
Grant us Your favor, and we'll be restored.

But now we're defenseless, we're wilted and dry.
We are treated as trash by all who pass by.
O God of great strength, O great saving Lord,
Grant us Your favor, and we'll be restored.

This vine that You planted, pick up one more time.
Restore us, replant us, remake us to climb.
O God of great strength, O great saving Lord,
Grant us Your favor, and we'll be restored.

Men chopped us; men burned us; may they catch Your
wrath.
You chose us, now keep us restored to Your path.
O God of great strength, O great saving Lord,
Grant us Your favor, and we'll be restored.

O God of great strength, we plead and we pray,
"Look down from Your throne; once more look our way."
O God of great strength, O great saving Lord,
Grant us Your favor, and we'll be restored.

Guard us and tend us. We'll kneel at Your throne.
We'll worship You only; we'll be Yours alone.
O God of great strength, O great saving Lord,
Grant us Your favor, and we'll be restored.

Psalm 81

REMEMBER

Sing for joy and raise a shout. Play a song and tell about
This gladsome feast, yes, celebrate! For God's ordained
this special date:

"In Egypt's land, as I passed through, I heard you cry and
rescued you,
Relieved your load, removed your chains, and tested you
at Meribah's plains.

"Hear me now, as I remind; have no strange gods of any
kind.
I am your God; I am your Source. I fill your mouth; I
guide your course.

"You didn't hear; you didn't obey. Your stubborn heart
just walked away.
If you would hear; if you would turn, your foes would
feel my anger burn.

"The ones who in pretense obey will meet their doom,
their judgment day.
But you, I'll feed with wheat and rye and honey meant to
satisfy."

Psalm 82

The Righteous Judge

God takes His stand among His own and judges every court:
"Why do you favor wicked men and of the poor make sport?

"Take care to note the orphaned ones and come to their defense.
Yes, guard the weak and needy ones from evil man's intents.

"They do not grasp the facts of life; they cannot understand.
The ground they walk is on the move; it's always shifting sand.

"Do you assume that in your power you never will face death?
Will you not die like other men and draw your final breath?"

The Judge of judges comes to rule; He'll take no bribing nudge.
Each nation and each man will stand before the Righteous Judge.

Psalm 83

BRING AN END TO ENEMIES

O God of heaven,
Don't stay quiet.
Don't stay silent,
Don't stay still!
Our enemies war;
They exalt themselves
And execute plans
To steal and kill.

They plot to come
Disgrace Your church,
Displace Your folk,
Erase Your name.
From all around
They band together,
Demand our death
And plan our shame.

Like Jael's tent,
Woo in our foes,
Then end their plans
And seal their doom.
Spread them around
Like dung on the ground,
Or hung by the neck,
Or flung from the tomb.

Then like a storm,
Blow them like dust,
Or burn like fire,
Yes, burn like flame.
Fill them with fear--
They'll see Your face.
They'll ask for grace.
They'll call Your name.

Psalm 84

ROAD TO LIFE

Your dwelling place is lovely, Lord.
It fills my deepest longing.
My heart, my soul, my flesh rejoice.
In You, I find belonging.

I see a place a bird has found--
The swallow's made her nest
And sits upon the eggs she's laid--
An altar-nook her rest.

Whoever dwells with You, O Lord,
Is blessed beyond compare.
O King and God, throughout Your house
Are praises everywhere.

The man whose heart finds strength in You
Has found the road to life.
His soul can sing; he makes a spring
In the valley of his strife.

Like falling rain, the blessings come
And rivulets start to flow.
The man who draws his strength from God
Will see his blessings grow.

Give ear and hear my prayer, O Lord,
As You heard Jacob's prayer.
Acknowledge both my face and faith;
Be with me everywhere.

One day with You within Your courts
Is worth a thousand days.
One glimpse of You as You pass by
Makes pleasured lives passe'.

You are our sun; You are our shield.
You give us grace and glory.
We trust, and You prepare us for
Our part within Your story.

O Lord of strength, O Lord of help,
How happy is the man
Who puts his faith and trust in You
And lives to do Your plan.

Psalm 85

GOOD UPON GOOD

More than once, You've favored our land;
You've brought us back, restored our place,
Forgiven our sin, covered our guilt,
Turned away fury, and anger erased.

Renew us now, O God of our help.
Do not be angry or displeased.
Dispel Your fury, quench Your wrath,
And cause Your anger at last to cease.

O Spirit, come with refreshing life.
We'll frolic, we'll laugh, and rejoice in You.
Display Your loyal love to all,
For God's great promise has come true.

I eagerly wait for God to speak,
Announcing His people, His saints restored:
For Folly has fled, and Reverence raised
A standard of good in the land of the Lord.

Loyal love and truth unite;
What's right for one is good for all.
And faithful men respond with joy
As the way of heaven sends its call.

Good upon good, God grants great grace.
The earth responds producing fruit.
God's ways bring life as He draws near;
Relationships grow when God's the Root.

$\mathcal{P}salm$ 86

HELP ME IN THIS DAY

Lord, bend your ear, and answer me;
My miserable voice is weak.
Protect me, for I trust in You.
It's You, O God, I seek.

O Lord of grace, I call all day.
My soul knows You are true
And You are good and You forgive
The ones who call on You.

Abundant in Your faithful love,
O Lord, take time for me,
And hear the voice of my distress,
My prayer from bended knee.

There's none like You, no one comes close.
No spirit, god, or man.
No one can fathom all You do;
No one discern Your plan.

Every nation You have made
Will bow before Your throne.
Your deeds reveal that You are great,
That You are God alone.

Show me Your path, O Lord, Your way,
Your truth--my stepping stones.
And may my heart be singly Yours
Always before Your throne.

I lift my heart to give You thanks,
To glorify Your name.
Your great and faithful love Has come
And frees from deepest shame.

Arrogant men rise to destroy
And violently seek my death.
They cannot see the Lord of hosts
Destroys them with His breath.

Merciful, gracious God of all,
Faithful in Your love,
Slow to anger, full of truth,
Strengthen from above.

Show me favor, and shame the ones
Who crouch to make me prey;
For you, O Lord, can keep me free
And help me in this day.

Psalm 87

SPRING OF JOY

His essence--
    Of the secret place,
    The highest place,
    The deepest place
        Is far beyond what we can know,
        Is far beyond where we can go.

His entrance--
    For He loves to come,
    He's glad to come,
    For us, He comes
        Into our lives through humble hearts,
        Into our lives through thankful hearts.

His glory--
    He will show to us,
    His plan for us.
    His heart for us
        Fulfills the hope of Spirit-born,
        Awaits the consummation morn.

Then those who sing and those who play
Will join their notes, together say,
"Our spring of joy is found in you;
You are our fount of joy--
        It's true!"

Psalm 88

CASTOFF

O God of my help,
I have cried by day.
I have cried all night
To You,
O God of my help.

Let my prayer catch Your ear.
I have had pain and more;
I am now at death's door.
So please,
Let my prayer catch Your ear.

I'm remembered no more.
Like a man in the pit,
Like a man who's lost grit--
Cast off--
I'm remembered no more.

I seem to be dead.
I've no light and no spark,
I am deep in the dark
Alone.
I seem to be dead.

Your wrath is my shroud.
Trouble comes like a wave;
And wave after wave

Overwhelms!
Your wrath is my shroud.

You've removed all my friends.
I'm a man ostracized,
I'm a person despised,
Shut out!
You've removed all my friends.

Can the dead do great deeds?
Can they praise You above?
Can they sing of Your love
From hell?
Can the dead do great deeds?

My vision is blurred.
I have cried out for days,
Tried to lift up my gaze
To You.
My vision is blurred.

Why cast off my soul?
My morning prayers rise.
Look down from the skies
To me.
Why cast off my soul?

I have struggled since youth.
Is terror not done?
I have been overrun
By fear.
I have struggled since youth.

Your anger has burned.
Your terror destroyed;
I am lost in a void
All day.
Your anger has burned.

No love in my life--
My friends have moved far;
My acquaintances are
Unaware.
No love in my life.

Psalm 89

LOYAL LOVE AND HEALING STRIPES

Your loyal love--my ever-song.
Your faithful love for young and old.
Your loyal love--eternal-strong
Your faithful love is heaven's gold!

Your covenant word to David-king
Your promise sworn to David's seed
Fulfilled in Christ--miraculous thing--
An eternal throne, as You decreed.

The heavens praise Your wonderful acts
And saints on earth Your wondrous ways.

Though men may choose to shun the facts,
No man's so grand as Ancient of Days.

So greatly feared, we bow in awe,
Your Spirit ever faithful-strong.
You rule the seas with power raw;
You crush each foe, each friend of wrong.

The heavens: Yours! The earth is too;
The world, and all that it contains.
The north and south designed by You;
With joy, You made the mountain chains.

Your strong right arm, Your mighty hand
Designed the trusted, truthful ways.
Your people laugh in a fruitful land
And live rejoicing all their days.

You are good and You are strong.
You smile; good fortune comes our way.
Our safety, Lord, to You belongs,
O King, to whom we gladly pray.

You gave a vision when You spoke;
You chose a man from all of us.
You chose young David from our folk
And crowned him with Your oil of trust.

He was established by Your hand;
And undeceived, he stiffed the foe.
Those who opposed him could not stand
But all were scattered to and fro.

You are faithful, You are loyal.
Choosing men, You make them strong.
O King of seas, Your voice is royal,
Ruling rivers with Your song.

Christ will call You "Father First-Morn"
God-Creator, Source of earth!
You'll declare, "You are My firstborn,
Highest King of highest worth.

"My loyal love, I'll keep for him,
My covenant love forever and ever.
His children, I'll establish them.
His thriving throne will perish never.

"If his sons forsake my law,
They'll meet my rod, my chastening rod.
If they live by flippant flaw
And do not put their trust in God.

"I'll punish them with healing stripes,
My love will ever faithful be.
My covenant love is ever ripe,
My word, my faithful guarantee.

"By myself, I now have sworn,
His sons shall evermore endure.
His throne will brighten like the morn,
Ever faithful, ever sure."

You have cast us off, rejected,
You have spurned us and profaned us;
Scorned us like we have defected.
You have broken and disdained us.

When our enemies have approached us,
You have made us flee the battle;
You have plundered and reproached us.
Made our swords just empty rattle.

You have cast our victories down,
You have stopped our youthful games;
Thrown our trophies to the ground.
You have covered us with shame.

How long, Lord, this life, this breath?
How Your anger burns like fire!
Though we live, we live with death,
Knowing soon our lives expire.

Your loyal love--where has it gone?
Your faithful word in our hearts borne?
Our hearts are dashed and trampled on;
Our ways--our enemies mock and scorn.

Yet honored be Your name, O Lord. Let this be so. Amen.

Psalm 90

OUR TIME IS SO SHORT

Lord, You're our home; You've ever been home.
Before there were mountains, before there was earth,
Before the beginning and after the end,
You have been God; You ever are God.

You made us from dust; we turn back to dust.
To You a millennium is one day that's passed.
But we, just like grass, spring up and then wilt.
We flourish, then fade; we flourish, then fade.

Your anger consumes us; Your wrath so dismays.
You've opened our secrets; our sins are displayed.
Our days are declining; our years but a sigh.
Too soon it all ends; too soon it all ends.

All of our lives, just seventy years,
Our pride and our labor soon gone; then we die.
Our doom is approaching, each day ticking fast.
O Lord, make us wise; O Lord, make us wise.

Our time is so short; Lord grant to us grace.
If You show us love, we'll sing out our days.
We've seen life's afflictions; we've seen evil years.
Now, Lord, make us glad; O Lord, make us glad.

Let us see You work; let us see You save.
Let our kids enjoy Your goodness displayed.
Let favor, O God, rest on us once again
And prosper our hands; yes, prosper our hands.

Psalm 91

SHELTER OF TRUST

He who lives in subjection to God the Most High
Will enjoy His protection, ever watched by His eye.

As a chick helter-skelters to its mother's spread wings,
So a soul finds the shelter that trusting God brings.

I proclaim Him as Maker, Protector, and Shield;
I trust the Creator, to Him gladly yield.

He delivers from snares; He delivers from death;
He protects, for He cares. Yes, He grants me each breath.

You will not be afraid of terror at night,
Of attack in the day or an arrow in flight,

Of the wasting disease that silently kills
Refusing to cease, destroying at will.

Though thousands may fall near at hand by your side,
Yet you will stand tall, clear of mind, open-eyed.

You've made God your hope; you trust the Most High;
You escape evil's grope--ever live, never die.

His angels will back you and you'll overcome
Though lions attack you, you will not succumb.

"He holds to me surely, so I set him free;
I promote him securely, for he has known Me.

"I will answer his call, be with him in trouble
I will not let him fall; his honor, I'll double.

"I will lengthen his days, a just compensation.
He has chosen My ways; he will know My salvation."

Psalm 92

THE GOD-FIXED LIFE

Begin your day by giving thanks,
God's loyal love, your guiding light.
Then close your day by singing praise
For faithful acts of God's good might.

Throughout your day, let His music play
Through you, His instrument, inside-out,
Made glad by all that He has done.
Rejoice with both a song and shout.

How great Your works! How deep Your thoughts!
But senseless men miss every clue;
And wicked men burst on the scene
To quickly pass and get their due.

Yet You, O Lord, are ever high
While those you shun are quickly gone;
Their bones are scattered far and wide
While You live on and on and on.

You give me strength like a charging bull!
Your Spirit energizes me.
I hear of those who seek my fall;
Yet victory is what I see.

True men of faith stand tall and straight
Like redwoods tower toward the sky,
Their roots secure in soil of truth--
By Your great truth, they grow and thrive,

Producing fruit when they are old
So full of vigor, verve, and vim.
Portray, display the God-fixed life,
Eternally strong. Depend on Him.

Psalm 93

THE HIGH GOD

The Lord is in charge.
His robe is majestic;
His belt is strength.
His throne is enduring
From way before time,
And forever in length.

The world is established
And man can't control it,
Can't make it behave.
Its floods cause a roar,
Yes, a flooding tsunami,
An unstoppable wave.

The High God is greater
Than the surf of the sea,
Than the ocean that rages.
The legends are true;
Your rule has no rivals,
O God of all ages!

Psalm 94

FOOLS WILL BE GONE

Avenging God, O Judging God,
Show up with power, show up this hour.
Rise up, O Judge, yes, come, O Judge,
And pay the proud with Death's dark shroud.

How long, O God? How soon, O God?
Advance Your clock; the wicked mock!
They vaunt themselves; they flaunt themselves.
A tumbling tide, they gush with pride.

Your people, Lord; Your loved ones, Lord:
The widows hushed, the orphans crushed.
The wicked wink; the wicked think,
"God is naive; God can't perceive."

He made the ear; can He not hear?
He made the eye; can He not spy?

The nations rise, the nations fall.
Just one short breath and then it's death.
O senseless men, O foolish folk,
You cannot see! Why can't you see?

The knowing God, the seeing God
Knows all your thoughts, knows all you've sought;
But God makes right, and God corrects
The man who learns, to God's law turns.

God comforts him, God gives relief
Until the day the wicked pay.
God does not leave; God won't forsake.
His judgments true lead people through.

So who will stand and lift his hand
Against the wrong, the wicked strong?
Had God not come, had God not helped,
My soul was doomed; it's fate the tomb.

If I admit, "I fell, I slipped!"
Your love upholds; You're good as gold.
When doubts come in and cloud our thoughts,
You hover near, our spirits cheer.

Can a killing king fit in Your plans?
Can a death decree? How can this be?
They join themselves against the good,
Condemn to death the innocent breath.

The Lord my God, my Strength, my Rock,
No justice lacks; He pays them back.
Their vile harangues will boomerang.
They will be gone; God will live on.

Psalm 95

ATTENTIVE WORSHIP

O come, let us sing to the Lord with joy;
Let us sing glad songs with a joyful lilt.
With abundant praise His throne approach;
On God our Rock, our lives are built.

The mountain peaks were formed by Him,
The abundant seas, the fertile lands,
The laws of life, the way things are;
The God-King rules--alone He stands.

So come, bow down, let's worship Him
Submitting, bowing heads and knees.
Our Maker-God will come to us
In person, let us know He's pleased.

He speaks to us if we will hear;
Let's not be stubborn nor be hard.
For men of old had seen God's work.
God was their Guide; He was their Guard.

Yet from their hearts, they strayed away;
They would not make God's will their quest.
In consequence, God's anger burned;
They never found His place of rest.

Psalm 96

JOYFUL PRAISE

Make up a song and sing to the Lord!
Wake up, O earth, and sing to the Lord!
Blessing His name, sing to the Lord!
Proclaim His goodness every day.

Tell of His glory among all the nations.
Boast of His deeds among all the nations;
He deserves praise among all the nations.
Fear Him alone above all the gods.

The heavens displaying the works of the Lord.
Splendor and awe surrounding the Lord.
Beauty and strength in the house of the Lord.
The gods of the nations are false, not real.

O families of nations, ascribe to the Lord.
Glory and strength ascribe to the Lord.
A glorious name ascribe to the Lord.
Enter His presence with offering in hand.

Casting off pride, come bow before Him.
Men of the earth, all shake before Him.
The world He established, come stand before Him;
He will bring justice to every tribe.

Then all of the heavens and all that is in them,
The seas and the lands and all that is in them,

The forests and fields and all that is in them,
From stars to trees will sing for joy.

He will stand on the earth; He is coming, He comes.
He will judge all the earth; He is coming, He comes.
He will right every wrong; He is coming, He comes.

With justice for nations, care for all peoples.

Psalm 97

HIGH GOD OF GRACE

The Lord is in charge; let His name be known.
Clouds of mystery surround His throne.
Let the earth rejoice,
The islands give voice,
Righteousness, justice are His alone.

Blazing with glory, His steps are aflame.
The earth and its mountains quake at His name.
The nations will see,
All peoples agree.
The cosmos itself His headship proclaim.

Let idols be cursed, for they bring disgrace.
Do-nothing blocks in the Life-Giver's place.
When the Son is the choice,

The daughters rejoice;
And You are exalted, Most High God of Grace.

Hate evil; be free from the evil one's hand.
Love Jesus who died for your soul as God planned.
Glad harvest indeed,
When His truth is your seed.
Rejoice and give thanks as before Him you stand.

Psalm 98

RESTORATION

Sing a song to the Lord that has never been sung,
For He has done things that have never been done.
His almighty arm, His strong steady hand
Have sifted the wicked out of the land.

The Lord has made known restoration for earth,
Revealing to nations good news of new birth.
His love never wavers; his word ever true.
The watching world waits for his wisdom anew.

All the earth, give a shout singing out to the Lord,
Breaking forth into singing with praises galore.
With lyrics of praise and melodious strings--
How joyful the horns proclaiming the King!

The sea gives a roar; even fish celebrate.
The world with its rivers and mountains so great
Rejoice that the Lord is returning to earth,
Righting the world and restoring man's worth.

Psalm 99

HOLY IS HE

The Lord is now ruling!
With fear, peoples shake.
From His throne, He commands
And the earth itself quakes.
For those who believe,
He's known to be great!
For those who do not,
He still holds their fate.

May all give Him praise;
Great and awesome His name!
May all give Him praise;
Great and awesome His name!
The reign of the King
Gives value to all:
Righteousness, justice
For both great and small.

Exalt God the Lord
And bow at His feet.

There is none, there is none,
There is none like the Lord.
Holy is He, so much higher than us.
There is none, there is none,
There is none like the Lord.

Moses and Aaron
Were priests of Your word,
And Samuel called
On the name of the Lord.
You heard them; You answered;
You spoke from the cloud.
They kept Your commands,
Passed them on to the crowd.

God of mercy, You heard them
And met all their needs.
God of vengeance, You punished
Their wrong-hearted deeds.

Exalt God the Lord,
And bow at His mount.
There is none, There is none,
There is none like the Lord.
Holy is He, so much higher than us.
There is none, there is none,
There is none like the Lord.

Psalm 100

JOYFUL LIFE

Shout out all the earth!
Shout with joy to the Lord!
Serve the Lord all the earth!
Gladly serve Christ the Lord!

Sing it out all the earth!
Come with singing to Christ!
Know this truth. Mark it down.
It's the basis of life:

He's the Maker, not us.
That's the basis of life.
He's the Shepherd; we're His.
That's the basis of life.

Enter in through His gates;
Giving thanks is the key.
Enter into His courts;
Bringing praise is the key.
He welcomes us in;
Thankful praise is the key.

He is good; He is good.
Good to each; good to all.
He is love; He is love.
Loving one, loving all.
He is true; He is true
To each age, to us all.

Psalm 101

AUTHENTICITY

Steadfast love and justice too
Will be the songs I sing to You.
I'll walk the way of blameless men.
O come to me, my Lord, again.

Within my house, I'll walk in light,
And from my heart, I'll do what's right.
No abject aims before my eyes,
No wandering way, no compromise.

No villainous vice, no path perverse,
No hateful friend, no tainted purse.
I'll make no place for slander's lies,
For prideful heart, for mocking eyes.

Deceitful men can't be controlled;
No place, no office can they hold.
Each morning I will fight the fight;
To clear my sphere of evil's blight.

Now faithful men have I espied;
We live as neighbors unified.
Noble men will be my friends,
Together seeking noble ends.

Psalm 102

FOREVER-FATHER

O Eternal One, Everlasting One,
Hear my prayer, O, hear my cry!
Don't turn away on this troubling day,
But bend Your ear to my deep sigh.

My days like smoke are blown away;
My bones like wood charred in the fire;
My heart is dry like wilted grass;
I do not eat; I've lost desire.

I'm skin and bones, a starving soul;
I cannot sleep, I mourn alone.
A seagull lost in desert sands,
A lonely bird, I moan and groan.

I'm taunted, haunted all day long;
My mockers fill the air with jeers.
My food is spiced with dirt and ash;
My drink is mingled with my tears.

In indignation and in wrath,
You've snatched me, slung me far away.
Like grass that never sees the light,
I pale as shadows rule my day.

But You abide, Your name endures;
Have pity; wash away our grime.

Once more build up, once more make glad;
Yes, have compassion. It is time!

Let nations fear Your name, O Lord.
And all Your glory, let kings see.
You'll build and bond believing hearts.
Step in Your Story; set them free.

The prayer of the lost, You won't despise,
As prisoners groan their death-doomed cry.
They'll speak Your name and sing Your praise.
They'll gladly serve and catch Your eye.

The longer I live, the weaker my strength.
The longer I live, the shorter my days.
O Father God, don't cut life short!
How much we need Your lasting ways.

You made the earth, the heavens too;
And though they perish, You endure.
Like clothing they will all wear out,
Like passing fads, become obscure.

Forever-Father, You don't change,
O Everlasting Cornerstone!
And those who serve You will endure--
Their children thriving 'round Your throne.

Psalm 103

ABUNDANT BLESSINGS

O soul of mine, bless God Most High.
From deep within me bless His name.
O soul, bless God the Lord Most High;
For all He's done, declare His fame.

Forgiving One, forgiving sins.
The Healing One, He deeply heals.
Reviving One, He leans toward me
And lifts me up--His grace reveals.

With loving touch, He crowns my life;
With good, my years He satisfies.
When I am down, He gives new strength
And lifts me where the eagle flies.

God helps the weak, He helps the poor;
He does things well, does all things well.
His goodness Moses understood;
His strength revealed to Israel.

The Lord bends down and touches us
Abounding in His steadfast love.
His anger slowly grows, then goes
To work His justice from above.

His love for those who fear Him most
Erases pain, erases sin.

From farthest star to lowest earth,
He reaches out to sons of men.

As far as east is from the west
So far He takes our sins away.
His Father's heart, His Father's touch
Transforms our darkest night to day.

He knows our flesh, that we are dust,
That we like flowers bud and bloom,
That hard life-winds will blow us down
'Til all that's left is death and gloom.

His loyal love is ever-strong
And passed along to children too,
If we will live in covenant love
And to His covenant ways stay true.

The Lord has set His throne on high
And He is sovereign over all.
His angels bless Him, do His will,
With mighty strength obey His call.

All heavenly hosts, come bless the Lord;
Come serve Him, walking out your roles.
I, too, join in with all His works.
O bless Him, praise Him, O my soul!

Psalm 104

CREATION PRAISE

O my soul, bless the Lord who is great beyond thought,
Who exists far above the great cosmic span,
Whose splendor can only be glimpsed from afar,
Whose storms and volcanoes are working His plan.

The glories of galaxies cannot compare:
They hint of His brightness, mere wisps of His flair.
He established the earth, set its orbit in space,
Marked out its course, and fixed it in place.

At first all the earth was liquid and gas.
Then He spoke, and rumblings and tumblings began;
With violent force the mountains arose
Dividing the earth, splitting waters from land.

Springs rose in the valleys and flowed into streams,
Gave drink to the beasts, made dry throats wet.
The waters of heaven so satisfied earth
That donkeys and birds were singing duets.

He made the grass to grow for the cows
And abundant crops for the farmer's table;
Wine for his heart and oil for his face,
Good food to sustain and keep him able.

Each tree in its place where its roots draw and drink;
And the stork finds its branches a place for its nest.

The mountain goats live on high mountain crags
While the cliffs are the home where the rock badgers
rest.

The moon phase, the sunsets are certain each day,
As dusk becomes night when the beasts seek their prey.
The young lions roar finding food from God's hand;
Then they lie down to rest, leaving daylight for man.

How wise are Your works, Lord. How ordered, how sure!
And the earth in its fullness forever is Yours.
The sea great and broad--how the fish mesmerize
By their features, their colors, their great monstrous
size.

They all look to You to provide, to sustain;
You give and they eat, by Your hand satisfied.
When You hide and withhold, and You break the food
chain,
They starve, disappear, and the species will die.

But Your creative Spirit is active again
Creating and shaping and forming anew!
May Your goodness, O God, forever endure
As You ever rejoice in all that You do.

One glance at the earth, it trembles, it shakes;
One touch on a mount; it burns and it smokes.
May it be so with sinners, 'til they are consumed,
'Til the earth is set free from the world's wicked folk.

As long as I live, I will sing of the Lord,
With all of my breath, proclaiming His praise.
Let my thoughts, meditations glorify Him
Increasing my gladness all of my days!

Psalm 105
GOD KEEPS HIS WORD

Be thankful to God and ask for His aid.
Help others to see what He's done, what He's made.
Sing praises to God, His wonders exclaim!
Be His, be glad, be good in His name.

His presence pursued: His strength endued.
His judgments declared: His marvels ensued.
O seed of faith, O sons of choice,
Earth's Judge speaks out with clarion voice.

Your covenant oath of Abraham's day
For each generation is newly conveyed.
The children of Abraham wandered around;
There was no place of rest to be found.

But the promise came of a home and a rest,
Of eternal possession where all are blessed.
God's anointed ones who spoke His word
Could not be stopped, were not deterred.

God stood in the gap and He was their Guard,
His will at work though times were hard.
He spoke a famine through the Middle East,
And food was scarce for man and beast.

He shaped a youth into man by pains
And formed his heart in slavery's chains,
Until the promise God had made
Came true for Joseph in just one day!

He was called, released, and finally free,
Made second command by the king's decree,
The good to reward, the wrong penalize,
To train even elders how to be wise.

He beckoned his brothers down to the Nile;
They multiplied numbers and strength for a while.
Egyptian hearts were turned to oppress,
To make them all slaves, to grant them no rest.

To undo Egypt's sinful blunders,
God sent Moses to work His wonders.

Waters of blood and darkness deep,
Swarms of flies, and frogs in heaps.
Ubiquitous gnats, destroying hail
That shattered trees on a massive scale.

Clouds of locusts ate everything green,
Chewed up the crops and picked them clean.
The final blow was first-born death
When Egypt's future lost its breath.

Then the people of God, free of Egypt's hold
Were told to leave, given tokens of gold.
Egypt was glad to see them depart
For the fear of God had struck her heart.

God shaded them as they traveled by day
And illumined by fire their nightly way.

They asked for meat; He brought them quail.
On heavenly bread they were hardy and hale.
He split the rock and a river gushed,
A gurgling stream broke the desert hush.

To Abraham God had promised growth;
He never forgot, He kept His oath.
He delivered this throng from Egypt's grip,
A joyful flock with a hop and a skip.

The harvest that other nations had planted,
The lands those nations had taken for granted
God gave to Hebrews, newly alive
That they might prosper, that they might thrive
To keep His ways in this chosen place,
To live as a people before God's face.

Praise and honor and reverence the Lord
Who keeps His oath, who keeps His word!

Psalm 106

FAITHFUL GOD; UNFAITHFUL MAN

Honor the Lord any way that you can;
Multiply thanks again and again.
He is strong in His goodness,
The same through and through,
Never ending His kindness,
Always faithful and true.

Words cannot wield the worth of His name,
Man cannot fathom the reach of His fame.
How joyful the man whose judgments are just
Who honors God's likeness in beings of dust.
Whose actions consistently demonstrate light ,
Who bends for the lowly and stands for the right.

Favor me, Lord, when You look toward Your nation;
Visit me, Lord, with Your mighty salvation
That I may observe the effect of Your choice
And along with Your people sing and rejoice.

Like our fathers, we've sinned; for they wickedly walked.
Although freed through the sea, they rebelled and they
balked.
God still made them His--His people, His own--
To show them His love, let His power be known.
He delivered, He freed them from slavery's land,
And He snatched them out of their enemy's hand.

They saw the Egyptians all washed away,
They believed God's words and sang His praise.
But they forgot His works, they forgot His will.
The god "Desire" possessed them still.
They pled for meat; God met their whim
Yet death came soon in sickness grim.

Abiram rebelled against Moses' lead,
Moses asked God to intercede.
Abiram was swallowed by an earth-quake hole;
And fire burned all who supported his role.

They worshipped a calf, a mere facade,
Degrading themselves, the image of God.
They set God aside, forgot all He'd done
And all would have died but were saved by just one:
Moses the chosen stood willing to die,
A picture of Christ who would be crucified.

When they came to the bounds of the promised land,
They did not trust what God had planned,
But grumbled and mumbled within their tents
Despising God's word, His kind intents.

They held unbelief; God's oath became curse.
They didn't know things would get even worse.
But they died in the desert, without a homeland;
No rest for the ones who despised God's plan.

They corrupted themselves with sex-god Baal;
They ate of the food that was offered to hell.
They provoked God's wrath with their faithless deeds

'Til a plague of death knocked them to their knees.
Then Phineas stopped it with his righteous spear,
And his deed is retold from year to year.

They provoked God's wrath at Meribah's pool
Rejecting God's Spirit, His benevolent rule,
'Til Moses in anger ignored God's yoke:
He struck the rock when he should have just spoke.

His people went on to conquer the land
But failed to cleanse it as God had planned.
They married with pagans, adopting their way;
They worshipped their idols and cast God away.

They sacrificed children like the Canaanites,
Spilled innocent blood in demonic rites.
They became so unclean in all of their deeds
That God's anger boiled, but they could not see
'Til their enemies came and took control
Abusing their bodies, oppressing their souls.
They were ruled by the nations that hated their guts,
For their vision was blurred; their path became ruts.

Though God would deliver, their thinking was skewed;
Their perspective on life was so misconstrued.
Yet He saw their distress, their whimper He heard;
And in great lovingkindness remembered His word.

He relented, redeemed with compassionate acts
And released from their captors, they began coming
back.
"Save us, O Lord, renew us as sons

To honor Your name as the true Holy One.
We bless You, O Lord; we praise and rejoice.
Forever we all praise the Lord with one voice."

Honor the Lord any way that you can;
Multiply thanks again and again.
He is strong in His goodness,
The same through and through,
Never ending His kindness,
Always faithful and true.

Psalm 107

GOD-CONNECT

Give thanks to the Lord, for He is good.
His faithful love is ever true.
Let the ones He has rescued boldly tell
How He set them free from their selfish views,

How He gathered them near from west and east,
From wanderings where they had no rest.
Their hunger filled, their thirst was quenched.
Let them thank the Lord for the way He's blessed.

There were those who lived in the shadow of death,
They were helpless slaves in misery's chains
Because they spurned the truth of God,
Rejecting the words of the One who reigns.

He humbled their hearts with slavery's toil,
They stumbled and cried to the Lord who saves.
He brought them out of their deathly gloom
And broke the bonds that made them slaves.

Let us thank the Lord for His faithful love,
Who involves Himself in the lives of men.
He has shattered gates that were made of bronze
And the iron bars that have held us in.

Fools are rebels and rebels are fools;
Because of their ways, they suffer and die;
But God will deliver them from distress
If they will breathe to Him their sigh.

They starved themselves, they hated life;
They came to the door, the door of death.
God's word and His ways brought healing and health,
Raising them up, restoring their breath.

Let us thank the Lord for His faithful love,
Who's involved with us and shows up strong.
Let us ever give thanks even when we can't see,
And tell of His help with a joyful song.

Sailors have seen the ocean's rage,
The works of God in the wondrous tide.
With His word He stirred a stormy gale
To humble their souls and dismantle their pride.

Like a staggering drunk who had lost all sense,
They had no plan, no future, no past.

But at last they cried to the Lord of the storm;
He calmed all the waves; they were safe at last.

Let us thank the Lord for His faithful love,
Who's involved with us in our darkest hour.
Let us praise Him in the public place,
And remember Him in the halls of power.

He changes rivers into dry ravines,
A crystal stream into mud and rust.
If the citizens there choose evil and sin,
Prosperity ends in a bowl of dust.

Yet He changes a desert to a sparkling pool
And an arid land to a place of streams
Where those who were hungry receive their fill
And establish a city of hope and dreams.

They sow their fields, they plant their vines;
They gather a harvest of fruit and grain.
Their cattle increase, their herds enlarge.
They prosper because of God's blessed reign.

The unrighteous see and are mute as a stone;
But those who love justice rejoice as they sing.
If you're wise, you will listen and make this your own,
And acknowledge God's love the most faithful thing.

Let us thank the Lord for His faithful love,
Who involves Himself in the lives of men.
Let us ever give thanks and ever sing praise
And tell of His help again and again.

Psalm 108

FAITHFUL SOVEREIGN

My heart is steady; I will sing.
Lifting praises with my soul.
Before the dawn, I play my songs.
Praising God, my waking goal.
Praising God, my waking goal.

I'll give thanks from crowd to crowd.
With every ethnic group rehearse.
Your faithful, steadfast love is vast;
Your truth pervades the universe.
Your truth pervades the universe.

Be lifted up above the skies,
That Your great love I'll truly see;
Above the earth be glorified,
And Your strong arm will rescue me.
And Your strong arm will rescue me.

From high above the earth You speak,
Announcing with Your sovereign voice,
"I mark each nation, fix its role;
Assign each time by sovereign choice.
Assign each time by sovereign choice."

Who leads us on? Who guides our way?
If You forsake, we won't begin.
So go with us and lead the charge;

For evil cannot, must not win.
For evil cannot, must not win.

Men alone don't have the stuff
To make our foes all flee in fear.
Our strength alone is not enough;
Our courage comes as God draws near.
Our courage comes as God draws near.

Psalm 109

INTENSE COMPLAINT

O great Lord God of my deepest adoration,
Wicked men mock with malicious mouth
And spread their lies in this desperate hour.
Do not withhold the word of Your power.

They have hemmed me in with words of hate
And fought me for no reason at all.
I am kind; they accuse. I pray; they curse.
I do good; they harm. I love; they get worse.

Appoint them a judge, a ruthless judge;
And let their accusers take the stand.
Let their guilt be proved and the verdict clear;
May the prayer they pray never reach Your ear.

Shorten his days and empty his house:
For his kids, no dad; for his wife, no spouse.
Let his children be poor and underfed;
May they wander from home and beg for bread.

May his creditors come to take what he owns,
And strangers reap the seeds he has sown.
May his property go for a paltry bid;
May none be kind to his orphaned kid.

May his family die, his name destroyed;
May the Lord remember the parents' sin.
Because their heritage has no worth,
Cut them off!
Wipe them out!
Cast them from earth!

Let the evil deeds of his ancestral line
Come before God time after time.
For they did not remember to show faithful love;
They pushed Weak-and-Poor toward death with a shove.

His language was cursing; it's all that he knew.
Kindness and goodness were weakness to him.
His clothing was pride and it took control,
For it covered him up and devoured his soul.

Let this be the prize of those who accuse:
Who chooses to curse, for themselves curses choose.

O God, my Lord, deal kindly with me;
For Your nature is truth and steadfast love.

How I'm afflicted, my heart in dismay
Like the lengthening shadow that passes away.

I have gone without food 'til my strength is gone;
And my body has shriveled to skin and bone.
They reproach me, they shake me off like a bug;
Just wagging their heads, they pass with a shrug.

Help me, O God, in Your faithful love;
Let them see You act, and witness Your hand.
When they curse, You bless and restore my name;
When they rise, may they dress in robes of shame.

I'll express my thanks out loud to the Lord;
In the midst of the crowd, I will give Him praise.
For He stands by the needy in Rescuer's role
And delivers from those who condemn his soul.

Psalm 110

THE GOD-MAN-KING

The Lord God spoke to the God-Man-King,
"Sit by my side and prop up your feet
On the back of every foe you meet."

The Lord God rules with scepter strong,
His power shown through the God-Man-King,
Whose enemies cannot do a thing.

174

From the break of dawn, like morning dew;
Your youth will come and freely appear,
Your people gladly volunteer.

The Lord God will not change His mind.
He's made you priest without a border,
Forever priest like Melchizedek's order.

The God-Man-King at the Lord God's hand
Will shatter all the kings around;
For in his wrath, they'll all be drowned.

The God-Man-King rejects the pagans;
Their corpses fill the valley floor;
Their chiefs destroyed to rule no more.

The God-Man-King conquers the land;
He drinks from every stream he fords
And charges on--Victorious Lord!

Psalm 111

LET GRATITUDE FILL YOUR HEART

Mention the Lord with your pen, in your speech.
Let gratitude fill your heart.
In a crowd of believers or alone on a beach,
Let gratitude fill your heart.

Always around are the workings of God,
A pleasure to those who observe.
Revealing, surprising, inspiring--His works:
A pleasure to those who observe.

A promise to flourish is God's gracious plan,
Fitting and forming forever.
Weaving life's loom with invisible hands,
Fitting and forming forever.

He reveals to His people His working, His care.
His covenant ever endures.
He reveals how each nation has secrets to share.
His covenant ever endures.

His judgments are just; His treasure is truth.
His precepts eternal and sure.
His ways are a blessing to age and to youth.
His precepts eternal and sure.

His people set free from self and from sin.
Holy and awesome His name.
His covenant ever the hope of all men.
Holy and awesome His name.

The fear of the Lord is wisdom's source.
And He deserves infinite praise.
The way of the Lord, a life-giving course.
And He deserves infinite praise.

Psalm 112

HONORED LIFE

Fearing God, man is blessed.
Loving Truth, conscience rests.

Daring right, improving health.
Giving much, increasing wealth.

Raising children, faithful brothers.
Blessing family, helping others.

Choosing good, never fearing.
Lending joy, always cheering.

Remaining true when life is stark;
Finding light when times are dark.

Trusting God, steadfast soul.
Fearing nothing, living whole.

Winning favor though in strife.
Honoring God, honored life.

Villains watching, oh so vexed.
Teeth they're grinding, so perplexed.

Their desirings melt away.
Wishes wilted; plans decayed.

Psalm 113

HEART-SONG

Praise the name of the Lord,
Yes, blessed be His name!
From this time forth,
Forevermore,
Shout out His name--Proclaim!

Wake with a song to the Lord;
For he who serves Him sings.
God's ways bring joy,
The angels join,
Your heart grows wafting wings.

The sunrise starts the tune;
So rise and hum along.
Though heaven's ears
Can't hear its sound,
Your heart can sing His song.

Who else is like our God--
Forever-Strong-and-High?
He must lean down

To see the earth.
He stoops to touch the sky!

He lifts the poor from dirt;
The barren births a boy.
Full-throated now
With all you are,
Sing out His song of joy!

Psalm 114

CREATOR'S CHOICE

When Israel escaped from Egypt's hand,
From their foreign tongue and foreign land,
Judah became God's holy place,
His chosen ones: His kingdom's face.

The sea saw them and fled away!
What ails you, Sea, that you won't stay?
The Jordan River stopped its flow.
What made it stop and cease to go?

The mountains shook like butting rams;
The hills all jumped like frolicking lambs.
Why shake like rams, O mountains tall?
Why leap, O hills, with bleating call?

Tremble, Earth, before the Lord,
Whose love for man is underscored,
Who, for man, turns a rock to pool
And makes a fountain fresh and cool.

Psalm 115

HIS STORY

It's not about us; it's not about us.
We're only a part of His infinite story.
It's about His truth and about His love;
Our part in it all: to give His name glory.

Why do nations ask, "Where is their God?"
God lives in heaven and answers to none.
O why do the nations bow down to their gold,
Idols that don't do a thing, not a one?

Their mouths cannot speak! Their eyes cannot see!
Their ears cannot hear! Their hands cannot feel!
Their noses can't smell! Their feet cannot walk!
Those who trust idols are dealt a misdeal.

O people of faith, O house set apart,
Give all to the Lord and everything yield.

Yes, you who fear Him, put trust in the Lord,
For He is your help and He is your shield.

He is mindful of us, O people of faith;
O house where He dwells, He blesses us all.
Our Maker increases us both young and old
Who fear in His name, the great and the small.

The heavens He holds but the earth loans to us.
To fail to give praise is to be like the dead.
But we will acknowledge him forevermore.
His praises we'll sing; His glory we'll spread.

Psalm 116

WHAT CAN I OFFER?

I love God because He listened to me;
As I begged for mercy, He heard my plea.
As I laid out my case: A, B, and C,
He heard me and listened intently to me.

I was caught, I was trapped when pursued by Death.
Before me Death's door; on my neck was his breath.
So I shouted in terror my panicked request,
"Set me free! Save my life, Lord! Deliver from Death!"

The Lord who is righteous showed me His face,
His heart of compassion, His bountiful grace.
He came to my side; He took up my case,
And rescued me out of my deathly dark place.

My soul can now rest, set free from its fears,
My feet free from stumbling, my eyes free from tears.
I now walk with God, for I know that He hears;
I'll walk on His Life-Path the rest of my years.

Men are a problem, I've come to believe;
For all men are liars and love to deceive.
When godly men die, "Don't mourn and don't grieve."
For glad is our God their souls to receive.

What can I offer to Christ for His aid?
I can lift up the cup of the blood that He paid.
I can pay Him the vows that I've willingly made,
And stand with His people whose faith is displayed.

O Lord, I'm Your servant, the son of Your maid.
You have loosened the chains that kept me dismayed.
By Your grace, now my vows will not be unpaid;
And I'll stand with Your people who live unafraid.

I will offer God thanks with my heart all aflame.
In the courts of the Lord, I will gladly exclaim.
In the midst of His people, I'll shout and proclaim
Praise for the Lord, for His deeds, for His name!

Psalm 117

LET US ACKNOWLEDGE

Let us acknowledge who God is
And what He is like
In every country,
In every land.
Let us acknowledge what God does
And what He has done
For every people,
For every man.
Let us acknowledge how God loves,
And how He is kind
To every group,
To every race,
Let us acknowledge how God is true
And how He shines
In every age,
In every place.
Let us acknowledge who God is
And what He is like!

Psalm 118

OUR LIVES ARE YOURS

The Lord is good! To give thanks fits!
His loving-kindness never quits.
Let His people exclaim,
Let His priests proclaim,
Those who fear His name.
The Lord is good! To give thanks fits!

The Lord is for me; I will not hide.
With His valiant arm, He's at my side.
In my life's span,
I will not fear man,
Nor trust his plan.
The Lord is for me; I will not hide.

People surround me and mock and scoff.
In the name of the Lord, I will cut them off.
They attack like bees;
I fall to my knees,
Tell God my pleas.
In the name of the Lord, I will cut them off.

We shout with joy with all our breath;
For He disciplines us but not to death.
By His mighty right hand,

Exalted right hand,
His valiant right hand,
He disciplines us but not to death.

There is a door to the righteous life;
So enter in; be free from strife.
Thanks is the door,
And nothing more!
Give thanks galore!
There is a door to the righteous life.

The rejected One became the Christ.
The marvelous One, a sacrifice.
God made this day,
Rejoice on your way,
And blessings convey.
The rejected One became the Christ.

The Lord is God; He lights our way,
And leads us to eternal day.
Our thanks are Yours,
Our praise is Yours,
Our lives are Yours.
The Lord is God; He lights our way.

Psalm 119

ALEPH
SECURITY

Gain without guilt,
When we walk in the ways of the Lord.
Seeing His signs,
When we wholly hunt with our hearts.
Right is revealed,
When we walk in the ways of the Lord.
His order's ordained,
So diligently do His deeds.
Habits are honed,
When I walk in the ways of the Lord.
Shame is ashamed,
When I look in the law of love.
Happy my heart,
When Your laws are lessons I learn.
Secure my soul,
When I walk in the ways of the Lord.

BETH
WORD-KEY

Your word is the key
For a young life to be a pure life.

My heart truly seeks
For me to stay in your Life-way.
Your word is my gold,
And my heart's clasp against sin's grasp.
How I want to learn;
I'll always reach for what Your words teach.
My lips sing Your tune,
And my songs survey what Your truths convey.
Your stories are rich;
With full-throated voice, I retell and rejoice.
Your ways are my aim,
And my life-song for a life strong.
The key is Your word,
And the right minute? When I delight in it.

GIMEL
COUNSELOR

O Master, let Your abundant life
Flow in and out of me.
Awake my joy in Your law of love
With opened eyes to see.
I wander about upon the earth
In need of Your perspectives;
And pressed by life's incessant whirl,
I long for Your directives.
I've seen rebuke for arrogant eyes
Ignoring Your designs.
Take haughty brow and pride from me;
I will observe Your signs.

187

When those in power plan my pain,
I bow in meditation,
Delighted in Your storied strength;
Your truths, my consultations.

DALETH
END OF SELF

I lie face-down in the dirt;
For I chose my way, my name.
Now my soul is grieved and hurt,
And I fear my end is shame.

Remove the flaw of my ways
That I may choose Your commands.
O grant me the law of Your grace;
You hold my heart in Your hands.

HE
TRAINING

If You teach me, Lord, to walk in Your way,
I think I can do my part.
Give me a grasp of what my part is;
I'll do it with all of my heart.
Give me Your strength to keep Your commands;
I'll love it, I'll love it, I'll love it!
Draw my heart to Your stories of truth;
And train me not to covet.
Turn my eyes from vanity's lies;

I'll live again for You.
Your word is the source of reverent faith;
I'll bow in spirit and truth.
Step by step, help me order my life;
Remove all guilt and dread.
Make my heart a righteous heart
To rise in the end from the dead!

VAV
I'LL LOVE YOU MORE

May moments of Your faithful love
Come to me and rest on me.
Salvation by Your truthful word,
Come to me, and set me free.
Reproachers taunt and mock my goals;
I trust Your word to guide my days.
Your word of truth is in my mouth;
I do Your word and walk Your ways.
I'll keep Your law continually
Forevermore, forevermore.
And I will walk in liberty;
Your truth adore, Your world explore.
I'll tell Your tales and sing Your songs
To men of power and show no shame.
Delighted in Your sure commands,
I'll love them and make them my aim.
I'll lift my hands to Your commands
I'll love them more and love You more.

I'll meditate on Wisdom's ways;
I'll love them more and love You more.

ZAYIN
COVENANT VIEW

Remember, O Lord, Your covenant word,
Your promise that's given me hope.
It comforts me in affliction's lair,
It brings renewal there.
I remember Your ancient truths, O Lord;
In them, I strengthen myself.
Though self-important men deride,
Your truth is by my side.
This truth-desire ignites my ire
When men despise Your law.
This flesh-house of my own so longs
To sing eternal songs.
In darkness I recall Your name;
I keep Your law in mind.
Your vision, my eternal view;
Whatever You say, I do.

HETH
WE BOW BEFORE YOUR RULE

My hope and my trust for today is the Lord.
I have promised to keep Your words.
I have sought Your favor with all of my heart;
Be gracious through Your word.

I have turned my feet to follow Your paths;
To You, I yield my way.
I'll keep Your commands; I'll do Your will,
And hasten without delay.
Though cords of the wicked encircle me 'round;
I'll not forget Your law.
At night I'll rise to give You thanks;
Your plan fills me with awe.
The ones who fear You are my friends;
Together we're in school,
To learn Your ways of faithful love,
To bow before Your rule.

TETH
HOW TROUBLE HELPED

Like a favored servant,
I've been treated well
Just like You said.

Knowing right from wrong
And good from bad,
I keep my head.

I once went away,
Brought trouble along
And paid the price.

But now I obey;
I know You are good.
No straying twice!

My heart grew soft
In luxury's lap;
I turned from You.

Ignoring You
Built false ideas.
Now I stay true.

Trouble helped;
I saw the truth;
I keep Your law.

Your law outshines
The glint of gold
And silver's draw.

YODH
PURE IN THE TESTING

You've made me and shaped me with strongly skilled
hands;
Give me discernment to grasp Your commands.

May godly hearts see me and may they be stirred,
For I wait and I watch and I walk by Your word.

192

When Your judgments are harsh, I still know You're
right.
You are faithful in pain; You are true in the night.

Your faithful love comforts. Compassion arrives;
And Your word brings delight, so my inner man thrives.

May I hold to Your ways and with truth be employed.
May those who destroy by their lies be destroyed.

May those who fear God and know of Your story
Count me as one in their own category.

May I cling to Your ways, Your pleasure my aim,
Pure in the testing and free from all shame.

KAPH
MY BREAD IS YOUR WORD

Enable me, Lord!
I look,
I languish,
I long for Your word.

Deliver me, Lord!
I'm little,
I'm brittle,
I'm spittle to foes.

Help me, Lord!
I'm maligned,
I'm confined,
It's designed by my foes.

Revive me, Lord!
Almost dead,
But instead,
My bread is Your word.

LAMEDH
BEYOND

Beyond us, beyond the earth, beyond the universe,
Underneath us, in the foundations of the earth,
In the deepest secret of the universe
Stands Your word
Forever
Without changing!

Before us, You were faithful;
To us, You are faithful;
After us, You will be faithful.
From the very first generation of Adam
Until the very last breath that man takes on earth,
Your faithfulness is displayed in the universe.
Its order reflects Your order,
And every single thing from the smallest particle within the
atom
To the expansive galaxies beyond the reach of our telescopes
Follows Your intent,

Serves Your purpose,
Exists for Your pleasure.

Knowing this, yes,
Delighting in this
Has helped me when trouble has come;
For I saw that affliction also serves You.

I am determined to remember Your foundational truths,
For by them You breathe new life into me,
Personally.
And You create for me new beginnings!

For, I, too, am Yours.

Having searched out Your kingdom secrets
And considered the witnesses You have placed all
around us,
I ask You to keep me, protect me, guard me
From those who ignore You;
For they seek to destroy me
Because--
I think--
I remind them of You
Somehow,
In my small way.

Even if humankind could get it all right,
Solve all the problems,
Eliminate diseases,

Make everyone equal,
Clean up the pollution in the water and in the air,
Create a Utopia,
It would not be enough;
For it would have limits,
Boundaries,
Beyond which no could go. . .

But we were made for the beyond.
The God-breathed spirit in man
Would strain against the completeness of everything
And seek for what is beyond.

Beyond us, beyond the earth, beyond the universe,
Underneath us, in the foundations of the earth,
In the deepest secret of the universe,
Your word rules.
Dynamically,
Powerfully,
Permeating every single thing
And actively giving it being,
Upholding us all
Joyfully!
Jubilantly!
Without limits!
Your word!
You!

MEM
I LOVE YOUR LAW

Your law, my constant meditation.
O, how I love Your law.
My outfoxed foes are in vexation;
Obedient, I'm in awe.
My insight stumps all my instructors--
Your storied deeds the key.
Your precepts serve as truth conductors
And sages yield to me.
The evil paths I do not wander;
Your counsel they distort.
The charge You gave I will not squander;
I learned it in Your court.
Your gracious truth like sweetest nectar
Titillates my tongue.
While falsehood fails to satisfy,
Your truth-songs must be sung!

NUN
APPLYING THE WORD

Without Your word, I am in the dark,
Grasping, groping, griping.
But with Your word, the light is on,
Illuminating, guiding.

I've made a vow; I'll walk it out:
Loving, caring, serving.

When trouble comes, breathe life to me,
Encouraging, renewing.

Teach me Your ways; I'll gladly praise,
Accepting, learning, growing.
Without Your law, I spiral down,
Sinking, self-destructing.

Wicked men seek to destroy,
Battering, scattering, shattering.
Your stories of truth, Your stories of joy,
Reminding and inspiring.

I keep Your truth, receive Your joy,
Obeying and rejoicing.
I'll keep the course, apply Your word,
In living and in dying.

SAMEKH
APPROVAL

Double-mind, double-tongue, double-cross: I hate.
Law of God, word of God, command of God: I love.
Hide-away, safe-house, strong-shield: You are.
Protect me, uphold me, sustain me: I live.
Wanderlust, deceitful lust, wicked lust: remove.
Trembling flesh, fear of God, hopeful heart: approve.

AYIN
SERVANT

I am Your servant.
You have shown me to surely trust in Your largesse.
I am Your servant.
Do not loan me to other masters for they oppress.
I am Your servant.
Your righteous laws so solidly just are always true.
I am Your servant.
Unrighteous maws gag on Your words and misconstrue.
I am Your servant.
My understanding comes to me through Your stories.
I am Your servant.
My heart expanding as I receive and share Your glory.
I am Your servant.

PE
NECESSARY PAUSE

When I see creation's beauty, I'm in awe;
Each time I hear Your story, I must pause;
For Your word unfolds Your plan,
Giving truth to simple man.
And as one, they point to You as Holy Cause.

With open mouth I pant for Your commands;
Show Your grace to me with open hands.
Your word my constant school,
Keep me far from evil's rule.

199

May I love Your name as one who understands.

In weakness I am moved by man-caused fears;
My eyes then overflow with streams of tears.
Redeem my failing soul
And renew God-sent control
So this servant sees Your smile throughout his years.

TSADHE
INFINITE ARCHITECT

You are the source of the Righteous-Life;
And Your judgments flow from who You are.
Your witness in nature is set, yes fixed;
You are faithful beyond the highest star.
Your word is pure; I love it, adore it;
It ignites my ire when others ignore it.
I am small, so easily brushed aside;
I make Your thoughts my constant guide.
As darkness troubles, and fears oppress,
I find delight in Your righteousness.
I thrill and I thrive as I pause to reflect
On Your work, O Infinite Architect.

QOPH
BEFORE DAWN

I cry from my heart, O Lord, My God.
Answer and I'll obey.
I cling to Your witness, I keep Your words;

Just be with me today.
I rise before dawn and cry for help;
For Your words, for Your words I wait.
All night long in the quiet dark,
On Your words I meditate.
O hear my voice with Your faithful heart;
Renew me in Your way.
For wicked men would hem me in;
Your law they cast away.
Your word is Universal Truth
And draws You near to man.
From Eternal-Before to Eternal-To-Come
Your Faithful Word shall stand.

RESH
RENEW

Look at my weakness; look at my pain,
And help me remember Your law.
Stay on my side, my champion remain;
Renew Your active word.

The wicked evade Your solid truth
And run out of rescuing hope.
Your mercies have kept me since my youth.
Renew your faithful help.

Enemies enter; and haters berate;
Their treachery I despise.

They scoff at truth, Your word negate;
Renew Your proven course.

The bottom line of truth is You!
Remember my love for right.
Your righteous ways are ever true.
Renew your steadfast love.

SHIN
IN AWE OF YOUR WORDS

Leaders seek me as scapegoat scum.
My heart stands in awe of Your words.
I rejoice in Your words as discovered spoil;
My heart stands in awe of Your words.
I love Your law and I hate the false;
My heart stands in awe of Your words.
Daily I praise Your decrees seven times.
My heart stands in awe of Your words.
To love Your law is security and peace.
My heart stands in awe of Your words.
Your commands stir hope for salvation's joy.
My heart stands in awe of Your words.
Your stories of old I embrace with my soul;
My heart stands in awe of Your words.
You watch to see if I walk in Your ways.
My heart stands in awe of Your words.

TAV
DEPENDENT

Far too often I don't understand;
Hear my cry to know why.
Far too often my troubles expand;
Hear my plea to be free.
How often I see Your wisdom is true;
I praise Your sovereign ways.
Your righteous commands are gifts from You;
I sing for my glorious King.
Ready Your hand to enter my fight;
Your precepts I have kept.
I've chosen Your law as my delight;
Prolong my joyful song.
Keep me alive to give You praise;
Expound to me my bounds.
Too often I'm like a sheep that strays;
What cost to find the lost!

Psalm 120

WAR OF WORDS

In my trouble I cried to the saving Lord;
He answered me from His throne.
From lying lips deliver my soul,
From a lying, deceitful tongue.

What shall be done to a deceitful tongue?
What shall be its reward?
Burning, glowing, white-hot coals,
And pierced with a guilt-tipped sword.

Woe is me; for I wander and roam
And mourning is my home.

Too long has my soul had its dwelling place
With those that peace abhor.
I am for peace; but when I speak,
Their hearts are bent on war.

Psalm 121

GUARDIAN

Mountains awe me and then they draw me
To God the Maker of all.
He who made heaven and He who made earth
Is help for me when I call.
His guidance makes my footing sure,
An always alert ally.
Remember, this Guardian of His sheep
Never shuts His eye.
My Keeper, He is on my right
Protecting at all times

From things that charm, from things that harm,
From inadvertent crimes.

The Lord protects from evil's lure,
And guards my soul to keep it pure.
Whether in or out my door,
He guards me now and evermore.

Psalm 122

COVENANT HOUSE

When they said to me,
"Let's go to God's house
And be with God's people!"
I was ready.

And now I'm there,
My feet on Your street,
Within Your gates,
Inside Your walls,
O covenant city
With covenant people
And covenant laws
And the covenant God.

Every tribe, every clan,
All the adopted people

Come to You, O Lord,
To give You thanks.
For there is hope
And there is trust
In Your judgment
And justice,
In the rulership
Of Your house.

Pray for oneness and peace
Among all God's people.
May those who love You
Find true prosperity,
Unity and community,
The welfare of each
Increased.

For the sake of my brothers,
My friends and others,
I sincerely now say,
"Do well and be well."
I will seek the welfare
Of the house of the Lord.
I will seek the good
Of the people of God.

Psalm 123

MY EYES ARE ON YOU

Tempted to be down, I lift my eyes up
To You, enthroned in the heavens.

As a servant watches his master's hand,
As a maid takes note of her mistress' nod,
To the Lord my God, I lift up my eyes
To You, O King, enthroned in the skies.

Political winds are not kind to us.
Be gracious, O Lord, be gracious to us.
Our souls are mocked with public contempt,
Ruled by the proud, themselves exempt.

I turn my eyes to You, O Lord,
Until You are gracious to us.

Psalm 124

ALLY

"If God hadn't been on our side,"
By His people, let it be said,

"If God hadn't been on our side,
We'd be dead!"

The anger of those against us
Would have swallowed, gobbled us down;
In their rushing river of rampant rage,
We'd have drowned.

O, blessed be God who rescued us
From their ripping, ravenous jaws.
O, blessed be God who rescued us
From their claws!

Set free! Escaped! Like a bird from the net,
Free to gleefully glide!
Free, for the God who made heaven and earth
Is on our side!

Psalm 125

NO COMPROMISE

Those who trust in the Lord are like a mountain--
Immovable, abiding forever.

Like the mountains surrounding the City of Peace,
So the Lord guards His people forever.

Do good, O Lord, to those who are good
And to those who are upright in heart.

As for those who twist the truth and stray,
The Lord will tear them apart.

The reign of the wicked won't rest on the righteous;
The righteous won't yield to their ways.

Lord, deal with the doers of deadly deeds,
'Til Your people have peace in their days.

Psalm 126

FREEDOM

When the Lord set us free from our captor's grip
And brought us back home,
What an awesome trip!
We were like dreamers walking on air,
Laughing and shouting; gone was our care.

The people around us watched and observed,
"Great things God has done;
Their lives He's preserved."
Great things God has done; our future's renewed;
And our hearts beat the rhythm of grand gratitude.

HARVEST

Let our fortunes grow
Like a river's flow;
Let our tear-seeds sprout
'Til we reap with a shout.
Those who weep to and fro
With their seed-bag in tow
Will soon laugh with glee
At the harvest they see.

Psalm 127

WITH OR WITHOUT?

The Lord is a Builder
And the way He builds sublime.
Without Him, effort's futile,
And your work a waste of time.

The Lord is a Watchman
Always seeing each detail.
Without Him, guards are useless
And their watching sure to fail.

It is vain to rise up early,
Stay up late, and work 'til dawn;

When you're sleeping, God is working,
Giving, loving, on and on.

The Lord is a Giver
And, children, I surmise
Are his greatest gifts to those He loves,
His highest, precious prize.

Like arrows to a warrior
Are children to a man.
When strong they grow, they'll fear no foe;
And unashamed they'll stand.

Psalm 128

RESPONSIVE TO HIM

How blessed the one who fears the Lord:
Attentive, receptive, responsive to Him.
How happy your days, to walk in His ways,
To eat of the fruit you have grown with your hands.

How fruitful your wife, a garden of life;
Your children around your table abound.
How blessed the one who fears the Lord:
Attentive, receptive, responsive to Him.

Prosperity flows through people of faith
Who are one in commitment, a covenant bond;
And the peace of God is passed from an age
To the next and the next and the next and beyond.

How blessed the one who fears the Lord:
Attentive, receptive, responsive to Him.

Psalm 129
BULLIES

Since I was young, I've been bullied;
And I often tend to pout.
But this I say, "Though bullies came,
They did not knock me out."

Behind my back, they tried to tie
Me up in hopeless fear;
But God the Lord has cut their cords
And set me free and clear.

May those who hate the sons of faith
Be shamed by backfired plans
And die like grass before it grows
Upon the desert sands.

May banks not cash their checks because
Their business has gone lame;
God's blessing simply pass them by
For honoring not His name.

Psalm 130

HEARTENING HOPE

From deep within I cry to You;
Lord, hear my voice; Lord, hear my voice.
May Your ears detect my whimper-call;
To ask for help--my only choice.

Lord, who could stand? No one could stand
If You kept score of rights and wrongs.
Your infinite power and crushing strength
Surprise us with forgiveness songs.

I wait for the Lord; my soul expects
And hopes in the word He's borne
Like a watchman looks for day's first light,
Like a watchman longs for morn.

O people of God, put your hope in the Lord;
With Him there's mercy and love.
His abounding redemption severs from sin,
Reclaims us from above.

Psalm 131

LEARNING

O Lord, I have learned
I am not above others;
I act with respect
Even when I'm in charge.

O Lord, I have learned
I have limitations:
There are matters for me
That loom far too large.

O Lord, I have learned
To quiet my soul
Like a babe in mom's lap,
Not needing a thing.

O people, let's learn
Our best hope belongs
In the God of forever
Who makes us to sing!

Psalm 132

NEW NATURE

When David vowed to build Your house,
He stayed the course, went to great lengths.
He found the place to rest in You,
To worship You, to gain new strengths.
To such a place we come as priests
And gain a righteous robe to wear:
Your nature's grace, our clothing now.
We sing for joy, we live, we care.

Your word is true, for You are Truth.
Your word comes forth from who You are.
Your promise is but natural flow
From supernatural reservoir.
For sons and daughters evermore,
Your place of worship still grants rest
And strength for those who enter there.
Our needs are met; our lives are blessed.

Salvation is our clothing now.
Our song is joy; our faces bright.
The Dark is doomed and walks in shame,
For Christ is King and crowned with light.

Psalm 133

CONSIDER UNITY

Look around; take note. Consider unity!
How good it is, how effective,
How pleasant, how infective.

Look around, take note. Consider unity!
An anointing, "in the zone,"
An added grace, dissension gone.

Look around, take note. Consider unity!
A shared vision, a common goal,
A single plan, accepted roles.

Look around, take note. Consider unity!
On the job, with your friends,
In your home, make amends.

Look around, take note. Consider unity!
The same love, status-blind;
Shared hearts, shared minds.

Look around, take note. Consider unity!
A humble air, no conceit;
Honoring others, interests meet.

Look around, take note. Consider unity!
Like the Lord, self denied,
Ceded rights, yielded pride.

Look around, take note. Consider unity!
God's blessing, God's pleasure,
Exaltation, life forever!

Look around, take note. Consider unity!

Psalm 134

KINGDOM KNOW-HOW

Servants of God, stop and look!
Acknowledge the Lord; you know it's right.
Serve Him in your darkest hours;
Acknowledging Him in the light!
Acknowledging Him in the light!

Lift up your hands to His dwelling place
And give Him pleasure; receive His grace.
He blesses from His Kingdom-Now.
The Maker of heaven and earth knows how.
The Maker of heaven and earth knows how.

Psalm 135

AUTHOR AND ACTOR

Let the Lord be praised; let His praise abound.
Let His servants join in the joyful sound.
You who stand in His house, you who stand in His throng,
Let His goodness rise in a lovely song.

The Lord is great, and I very well know;
Above all the lies let the evidence show.
He does as He pleases in sky, earth and seas;
He blows forth the gale and the soft gentle breeze.
He makes vapors rise; He makes raindrops fall;
He makes lightning flash and the loud thunder call.
He gives life to man; He gives life to beast;
And he takes life away, both from greatest and least.

Kings rise and fall by His strong, mighty hand.
He divvies out wealth; He apportions the land.
In the sequence of scenes on time's streaming stage,
He's the Author and Actor in every age.
He judges with justice; and the wicked should fear;
Yet His love-servants find His compassion is near.

The idols of nations are silver and gold,
The work of men's hands, lifeless and cold:
No speech in their mouths, no breath and no sighs,

No sound in their ears, no sight in their eyes.
Devotees grow like them, their worshippers doomed
To end without senses in twilights of gloom.

O house of great kings, bless the Lord Most High.
O house of high priests, bless the Lord Most High.
O brotherly house, bless the Lord Most High.
All that honor the Lord, bless the Lord Most High.

Let the Lord be praised; let His praise abound.
Let His servants join in the joyful sound.
You who stand in His house, you who stand in His throng,
Let His goodness rise in a lovely song.

Psalm 136

EVERLASTING

Give thanks to the Lord, for He is good;
His goodness is everlasting.
Give thanks to God the Father of all;
His Spirit is everlasting.
Give thanks to the Lord above other lords;
His rule is everlasting.
Give thanks, for His miracles and wonders abound;
His power is everlasting.
Give thanks to the One who made heaven and earth;

The universe His domain.
Give thanks to the One who made sun, moon, and stars;
He is the Father of lights.
Give thanks to the One who sets people free
From slavery and from sin.
Give thanks to the One who leads day by day;
He is the faithful Guide.

Give thanks to the Warrior who conquers our foes;
His victory is everlasting.
Give thanks, for He gives as He promised to give;
His word is everlasting.
Give thanks, for He lifts us when we are down;
His grace is everlasting.
Give thanks, for the food He provides every day;
His storehouse: everlasting.

Give thanks to God who reigns over all,
For He is everlasting!

Psalm 137

PAIN

Far from home in captivity's cage,
We weep, we cry.
Our instruments hung, our songs unsung,
We sit, we sigh.

Our captors demand of us happy songs;
We yearn, we moan.
Tormentors taunt to be entertained;
We burn, we groan.

Exiled, removed, all alone, far away;
Remember, recall
Those laughing days, those joyous times;
Recount them all.

And deep in our hearts a hope still beats,
"There's more; there's more.
The enemy's end, his final defeat.
And joy restored!"

When others go through times of pain,
Don't smirk; don't flaunt.
But strengthen them and seek their gain;
Be meek; don't taunt.

Far from home in captivity's cage,
We wept, we cried.
Our instruments hung, our songs unsung,
We sat, we sighed.

Psalm 138

NEAR

I will give You thanks for Your faithful love
And yield my heart.
I will bow before Your dwelling above
And sing Your praise.

You make me bold with strength of soul.
Your word is great!
On the day I call, You take control.
Your name is large.

If kings of earth really heard Your words,
They'd give You thanks
And sing and praise Your holy ways
And glorious power.

Though exalted high, You hover nigh
A humble soul.
Beyond all proof, You stand aloof
From men of pride.

When trouble surrounds, Your comfort abounds,
And I am revived.
When foes attack, Your hand's not slack;
You save my life.

You stay involved 'til things are solved;
You're on my side.
You don't forsake the ones You make;
Your love keeps on.

Psalm 139

PRESENCE

O Lord, You know me inside and out:
When I sit, when I rise, what I think.
You know what I do, You know where I live,
An intimate personal link.
You know what I'll say before I speak,
And You know what I'll never express.
I've learned that You're near;
Your presence surrounds;
I'm assured by Your hand's subtle press.

Such knowledge is wondrous!
I'm thrilled! I am awed!
For my mind cannot grasp who You are.
Where can I go from Your Spirit, Lord?
Where can I flee from the presence of God?

To heaven? You're there.
To the grave? You're there.

If I cross the sea with the wings of dawn,
You're there, You're there.
Even there Your hand will lead me
And Your right hand hold me close.
In darkness? You're there.
In the night? You're there.
Darkness and light are alike to You.
You're there. You're there.

In my mother's womb, You shaped and formed
Each detail that I am.
There's wonder and mystery in every cell;
And I thank You for who I am.
Your wondrous works are on display;
I see and I'm convinced
That I am made by Wisdom's touch,
Marked by Your fingerprints.
The moment when the sperm and egg
Were joined by intimate hearts,
Invisibly, skillfully, You designed
And chose my intricate parts.
You wrote the code for my DNA
With traits from dad and mum;
And then with laughter in Your eyes,
You added traits just for surprise--
The print of my Master's thumb!
In earliest stage, my course was mapped
And coded by Your hand,
Your purpose written in my heart,
My life designed and planned.

When I glean Your thoughts,
I gain and grow.
Such vast and varied store:
Such vital thoughts more numerous than
The sand upon the shore.
There are those who hate Your infinite thoughts,
And ignore that You exist.
Their hands are stained with the innocent blood
Of those who can't resist.
They speak against You and Your ways,
They swear Your name for spite.
Because I love You, I hate them.
O ban them from Your sight.
My hate for them intensely grows;
They have become my foes.

Take a thorough look at my sin-stained heart
And cleanse my internal depths.
Then freed from doubt and selfish taint,
I'll take eternal steps.

Psalm 140

PERSONAL WARS

Rescue, O Lord, from evil men;
Preserve from violent thugs.
With evil devisings in their hearts,
They stir up trouble, create unrest.
With propaganda's poisonous rasp,
They've flicked their tongues like deadly asp.
Rescue, O Lord, from evil men;
Preserve from violent thugs.

Keep me, O Lord, from wicked hands
And from their violent clutch.
They've made a plot to trip me up
And wait with ropes to tie me up
With hidden net set in my way,
Snare after snare, day after day.
Keep me, O Lord, from wicked hands
And from their violent clutch.

I said to the Lord, "You are my God;
O hear my prayerful prattle.
Salvation-Strength, You've got my back
In time of fiercest battle.
Do not promote the wicked's plot;
But cause his plans to turn to rot."

I said to the Lord, "You are my God;
   O hear my prayerful prattle."

A slanderer finds no place to rest;
   May evil ever haunt him.
For those who try to hem me in,
Their words return to taunt them
Like burning coals upon their heads;
   May fiery pits become their beds.
A slanderer finds no place to rest;
   May evil ever haunt him.

Righteous men who help the weak
   Display Your mercy's essence.
For You with mercy look upon
   The ones who are afflicted
And see that those who harm the poor
   Will one day be convicted.
Righteous men who help the weak
   Display Your mercy's essence.
Forever they'll give thanks to You
While dwelling in Your presence.

Psalm 141

SAFE IN YOUR HANDS

O Lord, quickly come!
My prayers quickly rise.
Muzzle my mouth
So I will be wise.
Keep me from evil,
From those who would cheat,
From wicked attractions
And poisonous sweets.

Let men who love me
Correct me, reprove me.
I'll take it as healing
And let their words move me.
Unlike the wicked
So full of disdain,
Despising good counsel
And counting it vain.

I make my words pleasant;
Softly I speak.
They plow such words under
And treat them as weak.
As bowling ball
Thunders and scatters the pins,

Their goal is to shatter
My bones in the end.

My eyes are toward You;
It only makes sense.
I've no better refuge,
No better defense.
Keep me from traps
With jaws open wide,
From snares that are set
For my homicide.

Let the wicked be caught
In their own wicked plans
And gaze as I pass
Kept safe in Your hands.

Psalm 142

DRIFTWOOD

Sometimes I need Your help on the double.
I complain, I get loud, explaining my trouble.
My spirit feels pressed and attacked all around;
No escape, no concern, no help have I found.

Are You not my refuge? The secret of Life?
Have You turned a deaf ear, ignoring my strife?

Life's ocean is huge, and its waves far too strong.
I have drifted ashore and been left here too long.
Come walk down the beach; pick me up from the sand,
Create of me something anew from Your hand.

Psalm 143

A SPARK OF HOPE

Hear me, O Lord;
Bend near in my stress.
Answer me, Lord,
In Your great faithfulness.
Judge me not, Lord,
In Your sight, I can't stand.
Only Your Son,
Is the one perfect Man.

The enemy came,
And I barely survived.
All became dark,
I was buried alive.
Defeated and whipped,
My spirit depressed.
Despairing, my soul
Could never get rest.

An inkling of hope,
A memory clear:
How You helped in the past,
A far distant year.
Because of this trace,
This small, tiny spark,
I reach out to You,
My light in the dark.

Answer me, Lord,
My spirit is weak.
Death is so near,
I dare not to speak.
My trust is in You
That I may see day.
Protect me and frighten
The wicked away.

Teach me, O Lord,
How to walk, how to live,
How to make out Your will,
To serve and to give.
O Spirit of God,
Free me from Satan's wrath.
Good Spirit of God,
Lead me well on Your path.

Psalm 144

WAR AND PEACE

I bow to Him, the One I need;
And others follow when I lead.

The Lord is my Rock, my mentor for battle,
My master to whom I yield.
Faithful in love, my fortress, my stronghold,
Deliverer, refuge, and shield.

We're merely creatures You have made;
Why ever look our way?
I'm just a breath that's quickly gone,
A wisp that's passing on.

Come down and touch the mountains, Lord;
With fire, blast off their peaks.
Dispel the foe with lightning bolts;
Confuse with blinding streaks.

From heaven's height, stretch forth Your hand,
And pluck me from the war,
From roguish men who know You not,
Whose hearts have rotten cores.

O God, my Song, I love to sing
And praise with strumming strings.

You aid the poor and make him king,
As David with his sling.

From heaven's height, look down on me;
Remove the evil hand
Of roguish men who know You not,
Who promise shifting sand.

Let youthful sons be mature and wise,
And daughters beautifully strong.
Let our storehouse be huge, secure, and full;
Its abundance enjoyed year-long.

No trouble or loss, let investments increase;
No riots, no need for police.
For we are His people and He is our God,
Happy to know His peace.

Psalm 145

FOREVER GREAT

I raise Your reputation ever higher.
I bless Your name forever and forever.
Every day I choose to bless You;
I will never cease to bless You.
I bless Your name forever and forever.

Says one generation to the next,
"The greatness of our God is beyond bounds."
We declare Your mighty acts;
Children learn your mighty acts.
The greatness of our God is beyond bounds!

We speak of Your awesome acts of power.
I will tell of Your greatness every hour.
Tell the stories of Your goodness,
Shout with joy for all Your goodness.
I will tell of Your greatness every hour.

The Lord is full of mercy and of grace.
Slow to anger, He is faithful in His love.
The Lord is good to all,
And His mercy's over all.
Slow to anger, He is faithful in His love.

Your godly ones declare Your acts of power.
Your godly ones proclaim their glorious King.
For Your kingdom's everlasting;
Your dominion's everlasting.
Your godly ones proclaim their glorious King.

When we fall, You are the one that lifts us up.
When we're bowed beneath our load, You raise us up.
We expect You to provide,
By Your hand we're satisfied.
When we're bowed beneath our load, You raise us up.

In all our ways we know the Lord is near.
He fulfills our deep desires when we draw near.
To those who call, He's kind.
In all His deeds, He's kind.
He fulfills our deep desires when we draw near.

My mouth will praise the Lord now and forever.
And all will bless His holy name forever.
Those who love Him He enjoys.
Those who fear Him He enjoys.
And all will bless His holy name forever.

Psalm 146

HELP AND HOPE

Praise the Lord from deep within,
With heart and soul, profusely praise.
While I 'm alive , I'll voice His praise,
With every breath, full-throated praise!

Don't trust a governor, president, king;
With earth-born rulers, here's the thing:
Like us, they die and all their fuss
Is blown away like so much dust.

Content a man when God's his Aid;
He's Help and Hope for those He's made.

Forever faithful to creation,
And to its needy population:

To victims, He's justice.
To the hungry, He's food.
To the prisoner, He's freedom.
To the stranger, He's good.
To the blind, He is sight.
To the doubting, belief.
To the righteous, He's love.
To the orphaned, relief.

Join in, rejoice, shout out proclamations,
"The Lord surely reigns through all generations."

Psalm 147

PROVIDENCE

Make your mindset one of praise,
For praise is good and pleasant.
Ditch complaints, for where praise lives
Attractiveness is present.

The Lord will build His people up
And gather those bestrewn.

He heals the hearts of broken ones
And binds up all their wounds.

He counts the numbers of the stars;
He gives to each its name.
He fills the heavens with His clouds,
Provides the earth with rain.

So great is God with endless strength,
His understanding boundless,
That those who trust in Him will find
Their every fear is groundless.

The Lord supports my troubled soul;
The wicked, He defeats.
For birds and ravens, He provides
And for the untamed beast.

God's not impressed with natural strengths
And talents of our own.
What earns His favor is our trust
In Him and Him alone.

With thanks lift up melodic song
With instrumental parts.
O people of our God and King,
Praise God with all your hearts.

He ever strengthens our defense;
Our sons are blessed and fed;

And He makes peace within our towns;
He satisfies with bread.

He blankets earth with fallen snow
And frost with patterns bold.
And all is iced and crystalline
By penetrating cold.

He breathes His word and melts the snow;
Breezes warmly start to blow.
The earth responds to His command;
Spring has come into the land.

Though all the earth responds to Him,
With people, only few.
And yet He gives His word to us
And calls us to be true!

We'll make our mindset one of praise;
We'll praise and thank the Lord.
We'll ditch complaints, for where there's praise
We live in one accord.

Psalm 148

PRAISE WITH ALL YOU'RE WORTH

Praise the Lord from highest heavens.
Praise Him from the highest heights.

Praise Him, all angelic armies.
Praise Him, sun and stars of light.

Praise the Lord, O highest heavens,
Even that which is beyond.
Let them praise the name of Jesus;
Everything, to Him respond.

From the heart, from the tongue,
From the old, from the young,
From the clouds, from the breeze,
From the mountains, from the trees,
From the princes, from the kings,
From the beasts, from birds with wings,
From the depths of the earth,
Give Him praise for all you're worth!

He sounds a horn from His own lips
And honors those who give Him praise.
He establishes forever
Those who walk in godly ways.

For His name should be exalted;
And His glory is over all.
Yes, His name should be exalted,
For His glory is over all.

Psalm 149

SONG OF SUFFERING SONS

Sing praise to the Lord with a song that is fresh,
Singing as one mighty voice,
Lifting a glad-song strong and free,
O sons of the King, rejoice!

Rejoice in His name with dancing praise.
Rejoice with percussion and strings.
He reveals His glory through humbled souls,
The ones who have suffered, yet sing.

Let the godly ones exult in the light,
On their beds, sing joy to the Lord.
Let homage for God be in their mouths,
In their hands, a two-edged sword:
An edge to avenge, to right the wrongs,
An edge to punish the evil throng,
And chains to bind the kings by birth
Who ruled for self upon the earth.

Sing praise to the Lord with a song that is fresh,
The faithful singing as one.
To be with the Father when judgment comes
Is an honor indeed for a Son.

Psalm 150

LIVING PRAISE

Everywhere,
Praise the Lord!

Praise God inside the Holy Place;
Praise Him in a wide-open space.
Praise Him when mighty creation astounds:
His infinite greatness all around.

Let the symphony praise Him
And chorus that sings,
Brass and percussion,
Reeds and strings.
As the cymbals crash and echo along,
Let all who breathe join in the song.

And everyone,
Praise the Lord!

☙

About the Author

Keith Currie grew up listening to his dad sing songs and quote fun little sayings. He planted poetic seed in Keith at a young age. By her example, his mom planted the seed of God's word and a love for its truth. At age eight, Keith began to attempt to read the scriptures at the beginning of his day, often falling asleep in the process.

Through the years, Keith has expressed his faith as a young singer, would-be athlete, hard-working student, children's songwriter, youth minister, camp director, public school teacher, Christian school principal, small group leader, worship leader, associate pastor, and now poet. He and his wife Patricia also serve as parent coaches to a growing number of young parents.

Through his journey he has grown in his respect for people, in his understanding of God's word, in his ability to be a friend, and in his hope in Jesus Christ.

Keith holds his B.S. from Trevecca Nazarene College (now University) and his M.S. from George Peabody College for Teachers (Vanderbilt University).

A native of Columbia, Tennessee, Keith W. Currie resides in Mobile, Alabama. There he and his wife Patricia have raised their six children, and Keith has served as principal of Covenant Christian School for 29 years.

Wyatt House Publishing

You have a story.
We want to publish it.

Everyone has as a story to tell. It might be about something you know how to do, or what has happened in your life, or it may be a thrilling, or romantic, or intriguing, or heart-warming, or suspenseful story, starring a cast of characters that have been swimming around in your imagination.

And at Wyatt House Publishing, we can get your story onto the pages of a book just like the one you are holding in your hand. With professional interior design and a custom, pro-fessionally designed cover built just for you from the start, you can finally see your dream of being an author become reality. Then, you will see your book listed with retailers all over the world as people are able to buy your book from wherever they are and have it delivered to their home or their e-reader.

So what are you waiting for? This is your time.

visit us at
www.wyattpublishing.com
for details on how to get started becoming a
published author right away.

CPSIA information can be obtained
at www.ICGtesting.com
Printed in the USA
FFOW05n1423160717